A RAILWAY HISTORY OF NEW SHILDON

Front cover (top)
The six surviving Gresley A4s line up for the 'Great Goodbye' outside Locomotion, Shildon (picture courtesy Ken Hodgson)

Front cover (bottom)
Gresley A3 Pacific *Flying Scotsman* and Gresley A4 Pacific *Union of South Africa* in steam at Locomotion, Shildon (picture courtesy Ken Hodgson)

Back cover (top)
Railwaymen of Shildon (picture courtesy Beamish Industrial Museum)

Back cover (middle)
Early Stockton and Darlington Railway wagon at Shildon

Back cover (bottom)
'Steam' gala day at Locomotion (19th September 2015)

A RAILWAY HISTORY OF NEW SHILDON

From George Stephenson to the Present Day

George Turner Smith

PEN & SWORD
TRANSPORT

AN IMPRINT OF PEN & SWORD BOOKS LTD.
YORKSHIRE – PHILADELPHIA

First published in Great Britain in 2019 by
PEN & SWORD TRANSPORT
An imprint of
Pen & Sword Books Ltd
Yorkshire - Philadelphia

ISBN 978 1 52673 639 0

A CIP catalogue record for this book is available from the British Library.

Typeset in 10.5/13.5 Palatino
By Aura Technology and Software Services, India

Printed and bound in India by Replika Press Pvt. Ltd.

Pen & Sword Books Ltd incorporates the Imprints of Pen & Sword Books Archaeology, Atlas, Aviation, Battleground, Discovery, Family History, History, Maritime, Military, Naval, Politics, Railways, Select, Transport, True Crime, Fiction, Frontline Books, Leo Cooper, Praetorian Press, Seaforth Publishing, Wharncliffe and White Owl.

For a complete list of Pen & Sword titles please contact

PEN & SWORD BOOKS LIMITED
47 Church Street, Barnsley, South Yorkshire, S70 2AS, England
E-mail: enquiries@pen-and-sword.co.uk
Website: www.pen-and-sword.co.uk

Or
PEN AND SWORD BOOKS
1950 Lawrence Rd, Havertown, PA 19083, USA
E-mail: Uspen-and-sword@casematepublishers.com
Website: www.penandswordbooks.com

Contents

Preface

History books are mostly conjecture, opinion, half-truths and best guesses; that's the conclusion reached in my three score years and ten. I once watched a TV documentary about the Beatles and noted that the (then) three surviving Beatles gave completely different accounts of the same incident in which they had all been active participants. If, as in that instance, first-hand narratives are unreliable, how is it possible that some grand opus, cobbled together maybe hundreds of years after the event, could be anything better than a best-guess, regardless of the reputation of the author? If you also factor in writer's bias, and I include myself here, then historical truth becomes an unattainable goal. Indeed, the best that may be hoped for, at least in terms of historical accuracy, is that the reader gets an unbiased account of events drawn from reputedly reliable sources. Unfortunately, as noted with the Beatles above, this too is fraught with danger. So, is there any point in writing a history book? Well perhaps there is. While I contend such a book is not and cannot be 100 per cent accurate it can, nevertheless, paint a decent picture of a certain time, assuming it interprets it as accurately as is possible given the source material. The most important thing, from the writer's point of view, is to maintain reader interest.

Which leads me to this book. Over the following 200 or so pages I have tried to produce my 'best-guess' as to what happened in the parish of New Shildon during the double century of its existence. Where possible I have used first-hand accounts and, if those were unavailable, drew on the most reliable alternative sources I could find. Nevertheless, there are going to be unintentional lies and half-truths. That is just the nature of historical research. My main concern is that the reader might find the subject matter dull. If New Shildon's railway history comes across as boring then that is entirely down to me, because I know it isn't. It may indeed be the most interesting railway story of them all, and I can only hope that's how it comes across. In making it accessible to everyone, regardless of interest in railways, I have had to make compromises, particularly in terms of technical detail – and not just because I don't understand most of it. This, I know, will annoy some. My reasoning, for what it's worth, is that what you're reading is not a text book. It's my reading of the momentous events which produced the world's first railway town. More importantly, it's my tribute to the people who lived and worked there, those who made the town of Shildon what it was and hopefully still is. I hope they like what I've done with their story.

Not surprisingly, putting this book together would have been impossible without substantial and sometimes crucial input from others. I am particularly indebted to: Paul Jarman of Beamish Museum for access to its library and permission to reproduce some of their historical pictures; to 'Search Engine' at the National Railway Museum at York; to the Friends of the Stockton and Darlington Railway; to the railway museum 'Locomotion' at Shildon; to Jordan Hazell of Hitachi UK for the use of the company's IEP publicity photographs; to the Friends of the G5 Locomotive; to Durham County Council Archive; to Caroline Hardie of Archaeo-Environment Ltd for help and advice; to Teresa Lawson for letting me have a copy of her late husband's unpublished research into Shildon's history; to Ken Hodgson for his wonderful pictures of engines at Locomotion and his local knowledge of the Wagon Works; to local artist John Wigston whose impressions of early Shildon bring that time alive; to Ulick Loring, the only grandson of Robert Young (who authored the definitive Hackworth biography) who started the in-depth research of the Hackworth family in the 1960s I relied upon; to Jane Hackworth-Young who patiently reviewed the book and painstakingly pointed out the numerous errors I made, and without whose thorough knowledge of both her own family's history and that of the Stockton and Darlington Railway the book would be that much poorer. Finally, I would like to thank my long-suffering wife Maggie who put up with it all, helped with the research and contributed most of the best pictures.

Introduction

According to Palmer's *Chronology of British History*, the year 1825 was notable for the Cotton Regulations Act, which limited working hours for children; the modification of the navigation laws to allow foreign and British ships to trade on equal terms; and, in the month of September, the news that the 'First steam-locomotive railway opens: Stockton to Darlington'. The railway reference was brief and momentous, if factually incorrect. It was *not* the first steam-locomotive railway; steam-locomotive powered railways had been around for more than a decade. Neither did the date mark the appearance of the first publicly owned railway. In fact, public railways had been around even longer, some twenty years in fact. It was also not the 'Stockton *to* Darlington Railway' but the 'Stockton and Darlington Railway' and it really started at Witton Park a few miles west of Shildon. Otherwise the writer got it right. Nevertheless, the occasion *was* momentous. This was the first time that a steam powered public railway had been introduced, complete with main and branch lines, goods traffic and passenger travel and thereby a model for the rest of the world.

The *Durham County Advertiser* said that, at around 8am on that famous 27 September, thirteen wagons, twelve full of coal and the thirteenth flour, were drawn up the inclined plane at Brusselton, 'in admirable style amidst the cheers of assembled thousands'. Clinging on for the ride was a rough, in every sense of the word, cross-section of the local populace, hanging precariously from the sides of wagons and perching astride the wooden beams which acted as primitive buffers between them. Awaiting the wagons, on the far side of the hill, was the snorting 'steam horse' that would carry the train on to Darlington and from there to Stockton-on-Tees. The age of the railway was about to begin. Additional trucks, modified for passenger use, were attached to the train, one of which subsequently became derailed. In separating it from the rest of the train one over-enthusiastic onlooker was knocked down, and so became the first recorded accident statistic, involving a member of the public on a public railway. He would be joined shortly by keelman, John Stevens, whose legs were 'dreadfully crushed' as he fell beneath the wheels of the train's solitary passenger coach. It was not surprising there was going to be such injuries. The enthusiastic crowd had seen nothing like it and had no experience of the thrill and danger of railways. Many, indeed, turned up without tickets, jostling for space on the twenty, modified, coal wagons the railway had adapted for passenger use. By the time the train moved away the modified wagons were seriously overloaded; some carrying twice the number of passengers they were meant to accommodate.

The crowd gathering trackside on that historic day would witness something earth-shattering; the nineteenth century equivalent of the first moon landing. What had been, until recently, just waterlogged fields were now the centrepiece of the world's first publicly owned steam railway. It wouldn't be long before the same land became the world's first railway town.

CHAPTER ONE

A beginning

1825 S&DR coal wagon.

This is not a book about the history of Shildon. There are other books, including a concise chronology produced by the local Women's Institute, which perform that task well enough. Rather, this is a book about the railway community that grew up a mile or two to the south, which took the name New Shildon. New Shildon and Shildon have since become one but, in the beginning, they were distinct and separate entities. It seems appropriate, however, that before we chart the history of New Shildon, we include a few paragraphs about its more venerable neighbour and future partner.

The name Shildon derived from a combination of the Saxon words for shield and hill (scyld and dun), the shield in question being the dominant ridge to the west that 'shielded' the settlement from westerly gales, whilst simultaneously restricting east to west movement for weary travellers. The climb out of the valley of the River Gaunless on the west side of the shield was the first major engineering obstacle the railway engineers had to overcome. This part of County Durham was, and is forever, coal country. A Roman road once ran along the top of the shield, and it is not stretching the imagination too far to visualise slave-hauled carts, loaded with coal, trundling along this ancient highway heading for the Roman military station at the crossing of the nearby Gaunless river. Coal was freely available in the area. It outcropped on the surface and was used for fuel long before historical records began. However, it was harvested only where it became easily accessible. The dynamics and dangers of underground mining lay far in the future. The Roman legionnaires using the military road would have paid scant attention to the handful of scattered cottages which was Shildon in their march north. They were of little consequence to soldiers conquering Britannia. Coal was a fuel used by the invaders but there was plenty to be had in the north-east, and from sources more readily accessible than the Shildon reserves. Local exploitation would have wait until national demand outstripped supply, most notably during the industrial revolution. In consequence, other than the occasional cattle raid by itinerant Scotsmen, nothing much happened in Shildon until the turn of the nineteenth century, where our story begins.

On 4 September 1818, a group of Quaker financiers, led by the Darlington based Edward Pease, decided that the time was right to exploit the rich coal deposits in Western and Central Durham. Like the rest of the country the immediate thought had been to build a canal to connect the coalfields to the nearest navigable port, since canals were already the accepted highway for bulk mineral transport. A feasibility study had been carried out, supported by surveys, as early as 1813 but, due to the steep hills at the western end, construction cost was considered too great. Luckily much of north-east England was already criss-crossed by railways and tramways albeit mostly powered by horses, and the technology was proven. The economics of railways, as opposed to canals, therefore, looked more promising and Edward Pease of Darlington, with financial backing from fellow Quakers, decided to build a railway. The topography that had to be overcome and the sheer distance involved made this the most ambitious railway project the world had ever seen. The aim was to transport coal from mines near Bishop Auckland to collier boats waiting at the nearest navigable point, on the River Tees at Stockton. A survey was commissioned of the land the railway would need to cross. East of Shildon the terrain was flat, and a railway could be built relatively cheaply. West of Shildon, however, there were problems. Common to all the potential routes, unfortunately, was negotiation of the formidable Shildon 'shield'. Here a standing or worked incline at Brusselton (sometimes spelt Brusleton or Brussleton in early texts) would be needed. Plans drawn up at the time, by the contracted surveyors and engineers, provide us with a wealth of information on the nature of the land as it was before the coming of the railway. The picture presented of New Shildon, for example, as it appeared in 1820, is fascinating in that it shows there was virtually nothing there. Every feature you see today, the schools, the pubs, the shops, the industry and the residential areas were absent before 1824. The land that became New Shildon was just an area of marsh. New Shildon's rise, its (partial) decline and to some extent its rebirth was dependent on the railway.

As an operational centre for the Stockton and Darlington Railway New Shildon was not an obvious choice. George Overton, the original surveyor's, plans show that most of the area immediately east of Brusselton Hill was scrub and wetland. In fact, Overton so discounted the area he deliberately included a dog-leg in his proposed route to avoid it. One can easily sympathise with him. In winter when the streams which descended the 'Shield' were in spate the whole area flooded, rendering it impassable. Overton's route therefore turned north at the top of Brusselton Hill and followed the crest, thereby taking the railway much closer to Old Shildon than the route the railway eventually took. The original hamlet of Shildon, at the time of Overton's survey, was the notorious haunt of smugglers and highwaymen, the Grey Horse public house and a handful of cottages with a total population of less than 100 people. The locals were an unruly mix of coal miners, agricultural workers and weavers. It can't have been the most prepossessing place to live. A Darlington weaver's song dating from the time includes the lines:

The weavers are all out o' work
For the mills are all at a stand
The combers are all out o' work tae

And there's not a bit of work to be fand
Sea we'll all to stinking Shildon
For it's over wi' Darnton- in-Dirt
Sea we'll all to stinking Shildon
And the devil take Darnton-in-Dirt

Why Shildon was 'stinking' isn't expanded upon but the proximity of an area of marsh wouldn't have helped. It appears that, while there was little work in Darlington (Darnton), there was plenty to be had in Shildon – assuming of course you were prepared to dig for coal, because Shildon lies slap-bang in the middle of the south Durham coal field. By the turn of the nineteenth century, within five miles of the village, there were several working coal mines and the town itself sat astride an impressive and exploitable coal deposit. By 1835, there were at least 10 significant coal mines worked close to and even within the town boundary including Old Black Boy Colliery, Deanery, Shildon, Black Boy, Tennants, East Thickley, Adelaide, Shildon Lodge, Brusselton and Copycrooks. Two more, Dabbleducks and Furnace, opened in the 1860s. The most productive of these, ten years earlier, were the mines near Etherley and West Auckland. It was inevitable, therefore, that these collieries would define the railway's start point.

Edward Pease.

Overton had worked long and hard on his survey and the Pease family thought long and hard before rejecting it. Instead, in July 1821, George Stephenson was asked to carry out another survey. In theory, the idea was merely to fine-tune the most recent of Overton's surveys, the object being to reduce the overall length and hence construction cost, but Stephenson had other ideas. In carrying out his own survey, George was nothing if not diligent. He walked every inch of the route, making copious notes, before submitting his recommendations for change. He proposed taking a more direct route from the start point at Witton Park Colliery, near West Auckland, to the coast, allowing for the required diversion via the town of Darlington. The line, in fact, didn't need to go anywhere near Darlington. This was a pre-condition of the Pease family who lived there. The story of how Stephenson was recruited by the S&DR is well documented, most notably by Samuel Smiles in *The Life of George Stephenson*, and need not be repeated here although it has somehow gained the stuff of legend. Despite what Stephenson's biographers may have later argued, his name was already well known to the proprietors of the Railway before he ever turned up on Edward Pease's doorstep offering his services. Truth be told he was not the humble, uneducated and therefore surprising choice for the company's engineer he has since been made out to be. That he was poorly educated there is no doubt, for example, in his own,

George Stephenson.

less formal, letters he often spelled his own surname Stephinson, which is doubtless how he pronounced it. His level of literacy was such that it is likely his better-educated son Robert handled early correspondence with his future employer. Take, for example, this extract reputedly written by George, in August 1821:

'After carefully examining your favour I find it impossible to form an accurate idea as to what such a survey would cost as not only the old line must be gone over but all deviating parts.'

And, later:

'If it meets your approbation I would like as well to be paid by the day.'

Compare this with the following paragraph, known for certain to have been written by George more than four years later:

'Your letter by this days post has cut me most sadly how to set off to London at such short notice I do not know as I am hemmed in with so much business and indeed I am not in a state of health for such a journey however I must go Lord Shaftesbury must be an old fool I always said he had been a spoilt child but he is a great deal worse than I expected I suppose the Dutchman has been making the best of him...'

Luckily, with son Robert at his side, George just about got by. What he lacked in command of the English language he more than made up for in enthusiasm and dynamism, not to mention a natural flare for engineering. One of George's alterations to Overton's route involved removing the dog-leg Overton had provided to avoid the steep descent into the marshland east of Brusselton. George took the direct line, adding an additional incline. Brusselton incline was more formidable than that at Etherley and required a more powerful stationary engine. The cost of both engines was £6,200, and they were both manufactured by Robert Stephenson and Co. This was the first real contract for Stephenson's factory at Forth Street, the creation of which was facilitated by investment from the proprietors of the S&DR. The boilers were impressive for the time, 20ft by 8ft, and Stephenson included a clause in the contract such that their water supply would be provided and maintained at the railway's expense. The company therefore were obliged to provide reservoirs near both engines, the remains of which are still there today. The eastern slope of the Brusselton incline involved a

Etherley Incline.

Western aspect of Brusselton incline (showing original Stephenson stone sleepers).

steep descent into the rough pasture shown as 'marsh' on Overton's plans. This land, that would eventually accommodate the railway works, was famously described by the engineer John Dixon as 'a wet swampy field.....a likely place to find a snipe or a flock of peewits'. Before any work could begin, the landowner, a knight of the realm by the name of Musgrave, was therefore required to drain the land as a condition of the purchase. This local agreement would have far-reaching consequences for the future New Shildon since it provided a substantial area of dry flat land on which the railway's infrastructure could be created. The land beyond Brusselton incline was reasonably flat and most of the construction cost was incurred during the first five miles, which included an iron bridge, designed by Stephenson, to carry the railway over the River Gaunless. This girder bridge survived and is currently to be seen outside the National Railway Museum at York.

Whilst negotiations proceeded for land acquisition around Shildon, a 'stripe of land' for the trackbed, through the parish of West Thickley, was purchased, a procedure that would be repeated along the length of the line. Land purchase for railway construction would often be problematical and associated with ludicrous compensation claims by the landowners. By contrast, the impoverished tenant farmers whose farms would be most affected by the railway received little, other than a one-off payment for lost crops and an acknowledgement that all fences, bridges, culverts, etc. installed by the S&DR would be maintained at the company's expense.

Every top team needs a top manager and the S&DR was no exception. On 13 May 1825, John Dixon told the railway committee that Timothy Hackworth had taken up the offer of a senior management role at a salary of £150 p.a. Dixon, who was secretary and general dogsbody for the S&DR at the time, accompanied and assisted Stephenson on his survey of the proposed route. Dixon was also the company 'official' who initially approached Timothy Hackworth (wrongly referred to as 'Hackforth' by the committee) with the offer of a job.

As identified in the reports Hackworth was to 'come and settle on the line', particularly to have the superintendence of the permanent and locomotive engines'. For the railway company, this was their second most important appointment after Stephenson, as Hackworth already boasted an impressive railway pedigree. He had once been the foreman blacksmith at Wylam Colliery, and so was working there at the dawn of the steam age, at the very time when the pioneering experiments in steam locomotive engineering were being conducted. It has even been argued that Hackworth was actually the leading light in the design, construction and development of the world famous Wylam 'travelling engines', built there between 1811 and 1816, particularly *Puffing Billy* and *Wylam Dilly*, arguably the earliest reliable and conventional steam locomotives the world had yet seen, unless you include Blenkinsop's engines at Middleton Colliery which worked on the rack and pinion principle like some mountain railways do today. He was therefore an obvious choice for the S&DR. He had even been employed by Stephenson, at Stephenson's engineering works at Newcastle, for the few months which included the construction of *Locomotion No. 1*, or 'Active' as it was then known. It is said that Hackworth was the designer of that famous locomotive's coupling rods.

The future of steam when Hackworth joined the S&DR was far from clear. It is a measure of this uncertainty that the company seal displayed four coal wagons drawn by a horse. It was the intervention of Stephenson that changed all that. For this reason, particularly, George Stephenson deserves the title often bestowed upon him, 'father of the railway', because it was only due to his passionate advocacy for steam that the decision was made to give steam haulage the go-ahead. Having convinced his employers that steam represented the best way forward, when the company's railway bill finally gained parliamentary assent in 1822 its text made clear it was the intention to use steam locomotives for freight haulage.

Steam locomotive construction, however, was still in its infancy, and despite Stephenson's enthusiasm, the S&DR was naturally reluctant to commit. To keep their options open, the Pease family financed the construction of Stephenson's Forth Street works. The factory was named after George's son Robert, who unlike his father, was a qualified engineer. It is an indication of the level of trust between father and son that young Robert was handed overall control. Nevertheless, before the first 'travelling engine' had rolled off the assembly line Robert went AWOL, taking an ill-advised sabbatical to South America, and leaving his father in a quandary as to how he was going to fulfil the S&DR contract for two steam locomotives, both to be ready for work on the railway's opening day. It was fortunate therefore that George could turn to Hackworth. Despite it being more than a decade since Hackworth had worked on *Puffing Billy* and sister engines, the technology had advanced little, and in important aspects *Locomotion* was even inferior to the earlier engines, particularly in terms of boiler efficiency. Nevertheless, if there was much of which Hackworth didn't approve, he kept his thoughts to himself and threw himself into the work. Stephenson was grateful. It was largely on Stephenson's recommendation that Hackworth was appointed Superintendent of the Railway for the S&DR in the spring of 1825. He was already familiar with much of the work he was expected to undertake.

Even before Hackworth's S&DR appointment was confirmed, he was at work at Shildon, overseeing the construction of the stationary engines at Etherley and Brusselton; spending so much time at Brusselton that it became his contact address for most of 1824. The two inclines were a compromise the company was forced to make because of financial constraints. For the foreseeable future, they would be a thorn in the company's side, particularly in terms of traffic delay, until they were eventually bypassed in 1842 by a tunnel through the 'shield'. The first Brusselton stationary engine installed had a single rotating drum, which acted for both sides of the incline. Ropes trailing either side controlled the ascent and descent of wagons. The two ropes constantly snagged and as a stop-gap 'boys' armed with crowbars were deployed trackside to try and ensure coiling over the drum took place as

The two-drum incarnation of Brusselton's stationary engine (as seen in 1875).

evenly as possible. Whenever ropes snapped, which was often, the boys were expected to leap on to the nearest moving wagon and apply the handbrake, or if this looked impossible, to derail the wagons with heavy blocks of wood nearby kept specifically for this purpose. Not surprisingly, even in those far off health and safety averse days this was not considered reasonable practice. An interim solution was the introduction of a device called a 'cow', which was attached to the tail end of the wagons to derail them if the rope broke. Since this relied on derailing a line of possibly loaded trucks it left much to be desired. The chaotic situation improved immeasurably following the replacement of the single winding drum with two, each drum catering for a single rope on opposing sides of the incline. Even so, the rope once broke while transporting committee members, of all people, over the hill. Luckily the brakes were rapidly applied to the coach in which they were travelling before it had accelerated beyond the point where its primitive brakes would remain effective.

In the same year (1825) committee report that mentioned Hackworth's appointment, the name 'New Shildon' appeared for the first time, the name being applied to four workmen's cottages, authorised for construction at the foot of the Brusselton incline, for the use of 'engine men, carpenters and smiths'.[1] By the end of the year, five houses had been built, one of which became the superintendent's residence. According to Hackworth's son, John, his family were the original occupants, making the Hackworths the first permanent residents of New Shildon. Alongside the cottages a complex infrastructure of railways began to develop. The manufacturing and maintenance works at New Shildon began life as a small blacksmith's shop located at the rear of an open sided shed, capable of housing two steam locomotives; the first workshop on a public railway intended specifically for 'travelling engines'.

If the railway could function adequately with horse-drawn wagons, and indeed in the future often did, it was nonetheless the aim of the proprietors to launch the railway in a blaze of publicity, demonstrating the awesome and novel majesty of steam. In consequence, two locomotives, as noted, had been ordered from Stephenson's factory at Newcastle, each costing £500. Only one, however, *Locomotion* was ready for opening day.

The lack of a fleet of travelling engines wasn't seen as a pressing issue for the nascent company. Although half-hearted approaches had been made to other potential manufacturers of steam engines,

Heighington Station, where Locomotion No.1 was first set on rails.

it was obvious from committee reports that regular use of steam locos was still not a given. Steam locomotives were seen as dangerous and unproven. A request by a local colliery owner named Chaytor, probably Colonel Chaytor, a shareholder in the S&DR, who requested the right to run his own locomotives over the S&DR publicly owned rails, was rejected as 'not safe or precedent'.

The first day of operation is of course the stuff of legend. There is an oft-repeated story that there was no way of starting a fire in *Locomotion*'s boiler on opening day, whereupon a navvy produced a magnifying glass and tar-soaked rag, which he used to get the fire going. This has generated the fetching legend that the first official public steam railway journey was initiated by the rays of the sun. This seems unlikely given the importance of the occasion. Too much was at stake to leave such a trivial but significant matter to chance, particularly with the world watching. However, the tale may have its origins in *Locomotion*'s first real outing. The engine arrived from Newcastle around the beginning of September in three pieces delivered by horse-drawn wagons. It was assembled on rails near the current road crossing at what is now Heighington station and it is possible that it was here that the first *official* boiler fire was started in the manner described. Since the tale is apocryphal we will probably never know the truth. Regardless, however, of how *Locomotion* was kick-started into life it was immediately put to work, shifting the remainder of the building material needed to complete construction of the line.

On the penultimate day before the official launch, *Locomotion* took a party of railway bigwigs, including Stephenson, on an outing from Shildon to Darlington, the purpose being to ensure that everything was ready for the big day. The bigwigs were seated in a purpose built four-wheeled coach, called *Experiment*, which had also been built at Forth Street, Newcastle, and this was its maiden outing. *Experiment* was fitted out with opposing bench seats, with a table running the length of the coach between them. As the only purpose-built passenger coach, *Experiment* became part of the inaugural train on the opening day. It was destined, however, for just a short time in the spotlight, being employed for just a few months before being replaced by more comfortable passenger coaches. It is uncertain what happened to it afterwards, but the likelihood is that it was demounted from its wheels and the body used as a trackside hut, which is what happened to other early coaches on the same railway.

On that famous September day, it was the only passenger conveyance provided with a roof, so it was as well that the weather stayed fine.

With all the elements in place, and the stage set, the fun could now commence.

CHAPTER TWO

Opening for business

According to the *London Morning Post* of 4 October 1825:

'So early as half past five o clock in the morning, a number of wagons fitted up with seats for the reception of strangers, and others for the workmen, were fully occupied and they proceeded (drawn by horses) along the railway from Darlington towards the permanent steam engine, situate below Brusselton Tower. About the same time in the morning, several of the members of the Railway Company and their friends set out in post-chaises and other carriages towards the same point near to which had been determined the procession for Stockton should be formed. These latter drove to West Auckland, where a scene of gaiety and bustle was witnessed, surpassing perhaps anything that had occurred in that place before. Gentlemen's carriages, post-chaises, gigs, jaunting cars, wagons and carts filled with company, were seen entering the village from all directions, while equestrians mounted on spirited steeds and others on broken down hacks and stupid donkies, added to the general effect, which was still further increased by a vast concourse of pedestrians, who pressed forward eager to behold a sight altogether new in that part of the country.'

The first steam-hauled train from New Shildon left from a spot near where the Crossings public house (formerly the Mason's Arms)

Where it began. The starting point for the first steam train out of New Shildon.

stands today. It is unlikely there was a Mason's Arms at the time, more probably just a junction of highway and rails in the middle of a field. Indeed, it remains a matter of speculation as to when the Mason's Arms was built. The current view is that it was private accommodation for masons working on the railway, hence the name. It was certainly used later by the S&DR as a ticket office and general admin office as well as being the starting point for steam-hauled passenger trains. A waiting room for passengers was rented within in 1837, by which time it had passed into private ownership. It is also unclear when it became a public house rather than just a lodging place. On the face of it seems surprising that the abstemious Quaker proprietors ever considered using a pub for their office. However, it makes sense from a sanitary perspective, as thinned down or 'small beer' was actually safer than the local drinking water which was invariably contaminated. In fact the S&DR opened four other pubs along the course of its line and its branches. The Mason's Arms succeeded the Globe public house as the New Shildon railwaymen's regular watering hole.

In the 34 wagons which comprised the train (plus the passenger coach *Experiment*) seating had been provided for 300 passengers, a dozen or more crammed into bench seats within each wagon. Six of the wagons which carried passengers were also loaded with coal and another with flour suggesting the possibility of a select group of black and white passengers at journey's end. The combination of coal, passengers and agricultural produce represented a cross section of the traffic the railway hoped to attract. The passengers allocated with seats were far outnumbered by the unseated hangers-on. It has been suggested that more than 500 people travelled aboard that first train, many dangling from the sides of the wagons or perched perilously on the wooden beams between them which acted as buffers. Aware that the trackside public wouldn't know what to expect, for the first few miles, the train was preceded by a horseman, reputedly John Dixon, waving a red flag. However, by the time the train reached Stockton, the flag bearer had wisely moved to one side, after struggling to keep up. The coal was distributed amongst the poor when the train reached Darlington and, from there to Stockton, every available (and unavailable) space on the train was occupied by rowdy hitchhiking day-trippers.

Considering the enthusiasm shown by the public on the day, it is odd that the S&DR for some time after showed little interest in pursuing the idea of passenger traffic. It is a measure of how naïve

Opening day on the S&DR (from a later drawing).

the proprietors were in exploiting this aspect of their operation that the public for weeks after the official opening was allowed to ride on coal trains for free, provided they could find sufficient room and purchase on a wagon.[2] Eventually, enough was enough and *Experiment* was leased out for £2 2s 0d per week to Thomas Close, who set up his own horse-drawn rail service between Stockton and Darlington. After a few months, this loose franchise arrangement was transferred to Richard Pickersgill, who subsequently also provided stables for the S&DR's own horses. Pickersgill found room for additional passengers on the coach roof, as had been commonplace in the days of horse-drawn coaches on the highway. If you were too poor to travel inside Pickersgill's coach, you could always sit out on top exposed to the elements for the hour-long journey between the towns, for 9d. Passenger transportation on the S&DR was franchised out to independent operators for another five years, with *Experiment* ending its life, as it began, on the section of line between New Shildon and Darlington. In 1827, it too gave way to a horse-drawn coach, named *Perseverance*, owned by Shildon resident Dan Adamson. Adamson's coach house opposite his Grey Horse public house in Old Shildon, which is still standing, became perhaps the first purpose built public waiting rooms for a rail/coach service and indeed bears a wall plaque to that effect. At first, passengers purchased tickets at the Grey Horse then joined the coach at the Mason's Arms crossing until the private Surtees line was opened. Since the Surtees line ran right past the Grey Horse, in 1831, the pub/coach house became the new passenger terminus.

After the S&DR took over passenger transport in 1833, waiting room facilities were required in New Shildon. Problems caused by the 'shield' still needed to be overcome. Travellers from West Auckland were transported by horse-drawn coach to the western end of the Brusselton incline, where their coach was attached to a moving rope and winched over the hill. This presented a problem for those less fortunate passengers who rode on top, especially in the dark. In 1834, one of these unfortunate travellers gashed his head on the winding drum at the top of the incline. The coach's guard received an official warning from the company for not providing any lights during the hours of darkness. In New Shildon, the coach from West Auckland was linked to the tail end of a steam train waiting at the Mason's Arms to continue the remainder of the journey.

Less than a year after the opening, two men with foreign accents turned up at the S&DR workshops. They were there at the behest of the Mining Department of the Prussian Ministry of the Interior, who had given them instructions to assess the suitability of British railway technology to the Prussian state; instructions regarding which they applied themselves with the enthusiasm and vigour of youth. Karl August Ludwig Freiherr von Oeynhausen was 31 and his colleague Ernst Heinrich Karl von Dechen was 25. They were given a tight schedule and had to cram as much into the few months they were in Britain as was humanly possible. To this end they travelled the length and breadth of the country, dropping in on as many railways, both public and private, as could be accommodated within their limited time allotment. New to railways and unsure of what was important and what was not, they made detailed notes on everything they saw. This was ideal for us in that it provides a neat snapshot of how the S&DR appeared in 1826. The two young men were nothing if not thorough; no parameter was too trivial to be excluded. They calculated, for example, the average speed a horse could move three loaded coal wagons on rails (three feet a second) and the precise dimensions of the standing inclines at Shildon. They went so far as to pace out the distances involved to verify the information they had been given by the railway company, concluding that the length of Brusselton incline was 152 ft. 8 inches on the east side and 89 ft. 8 inches on the west with a gradient of 3ft. elevation for every 100ft distance ascent on the west,

Adamson's Coach
House. The first
Shildon passenger
station.

2ft for every 500ft descent on the east. They examined the structure and durability of the rails, applying measuring callipers to wheel axles and brakes, whilst all the while making detailed drawings of everything they thought might prove remotely useful. In doing so, they assembled an encyclopaedia of detail on the world's first public steam railway. While the Prussian engineers managed to visit numerous railways in their time in the UK, they nevertheless considered the S&DR to be 'the finest in England', to the extent that von Oeynhausen and von Dechen visited New Shildon on two occasions; the first in Autumn 1826 and the second just before their return home in the summer of 1827. It seems a lot had happened at New Shildon in the two years since opening day. The two inclines at Etherley and Brusselton were now fully functional and the first passenger trains were plying daily between New Shildon and Stockton-on-Tees, albeit that the use of steam locomotives was still confined to freight trains. In consequence, the S&DR was now internationally famous and a parade of foreign visitors was turning up at New Shildon to gauge the reasons for its success.

On the engineers' first visit to the S&DR, in 1826, the railway was still in a state of flux with the network far from complete. Even by the end of that year only the main line was fully functional, along with a short branch to the market town of Yarm and some feeder spurs to local collieries. In New Shildon, the company was still going through the motions of acquiring the land needed for sheds and workshops and this was proving problematical. Despite initial temporary agreements with landowners, land purchase had been a long, drawn-out process, even when the land sought had little agricultural value. Some evidence of the nature of the terrain the engineers had to deal with may be divined from their report, where they noted that the Etherley incline kept collapsing because:

'the swampy ground was not able to support the weight of the embankment, which continually sank and caused the ground to swell up at both sides'.

Regardless, New Shildon was now the centre of S&DR operations, and overseen by Timothy Hackworth, referred to in the Prussian report as the company's 'mechanician'. Six locos were being used, four described as 'similar in appearance and construction', and therefore probably the Stephenson engines: *Locomotion*, *Hope* and *Black Diamond*, with the fifth the ill-fated *Stockton*, which exploded spectacularly shortly after the Prussian visit, killing the unfortunate driver. Intriguingly, the sixth may have been an experimental locomotive called *Chittaprat*; the onomatopoeic name derived from the stuttering noise it made when exhausting steam. *Chittaprat* was such a poor performer it was eventually taken apart, with various components recycled as part of Hackworth's revolutionary engine, *Royal George*. The engines were noted by the foreign visitors as an improvement on horses in terms of their load handling, but their overall performance was seen as less than impressive. The average speed for steam-hauled journeys between Shildon and Stockton, involving 16 loaded coal wagons, was 4mph, rising to 5mph for trains made up of 'empties' on the return leg, slower in fact than the same journey by horse-drawn trains. In addition, steam-hauled trains regularly failed to reach their destination, a fact the authors diplomatically excused by citing the poor condition of the track, which mostly consisted of brittle cast-iron rails. In truth, the problem was the inadequate performance of Stephenson's engines.

John Wigston's artist's impression of a less than typical day in New Shildon, with Hackworth's S&DR engines *Royal George* and *Victory* either side of his Rainhill Trial entry *Sanspareil*.

In a telling letter to Timothy Hackworth, a future steam locomotive manufacturer William Kitching, then employed by the S&DR, lamented the state of Stephenson's locos:

> 'every Engine which they have yet sent has had great needs of mending, the new one last sent was at work scarcely a week before it was completely comdemd and not fit to be used in its present state, the hand gearing and valves have no controul in working it, when standing without the wagons at Tullys a few days ago, it started by itself when the steam was shut of and all that Jem Stephenson could do was not stop it, run down the branch with such speed that old Jem was crying out for help everyone expecty to see them both dashd to atoms the depots being quite clear of wagons, which would have been case had not the teamers and others thrown blocks &c in the way and fortunaly threw it off, a similar occurrence the following day in going to Stockton as soon as the wagons were unhookd at the top of the run away goes Maniac defying all the power and skill of her Jockey, old Jem nor could it be stopt untill it arrive near the staiths, had a coach been on the road coming up its passengers would have been in most dangerous stituation.'[3]

It was also pointed out, significantly, in the Prussian report, that none of the drivers worked directly for the S&DR but were merely self-employed sub-contractors, shifting materials for a farthing per ton per mile. Out of this modest sum, the drivers had to provide any coal and oil used, and pay the wages of the fireman, without whom the engines couldn't operate. The drivers were referred to as 'Leaders', regardless of whether it was locomotives or horses they were 'leading' and the rate of pay for horse drivers on the S&DR was considerably more than for engine drivers; this without the additional expenditure incurred from locomotive operation. The higher rate of pay for the horsemen may have been down to the tonnage a horse could move during a working day which was much less than for a steam loco, and there were many more horses than locos, some forty in 1830 compared to just seven steam locomotives, according to an independent auditor, Thomas Hall of Black Boy Colliery. After factoring in the greater damage caused by steam engines to rails, compared to their grass-guzzling counterparts, plus the expense of purchasing and maintaining the machines, the financial benefit of engines over horses was marginal at best or, as the authors of the report put it:

> 'On these grounds it may be difficult to ascertain exactly how much advantage, or whether any advantage at all, results for traction by locomotive engines.'

The Management of the S&DR were no doubt thinking the same thing. In consequence, the intervention of Timothy Hackworth, who offered reliable and efficient steam locos, almost certainly ensured the survival of the steam locomotive at this crucial moment in railway history, of which more later. If the Teutonic Twosome were unconvinced of steam's benefits, they nevertheless took the time to venture north to visit Stephenson's engineering works at Newcastle to see what developments, if any, were in the pipeline. What they found was an odd 0-2-2-0, subsequently trialled at New Shildon under the provisional but tellingly appropriate name *Experiment*; an experiment which ultimately proved unsuccessful.

If unimpressed by steam locos, the Continental visitors had nothing but praise for the steam powered inclines they saw, to the extent one would have supposed their eventual recommendation to their employers would have been for continuous-rope worked railways, as indeed they had noted on some small private operations. Even so, they also were aware that there were worrying glitches even in this technology. In the days before telegraphy, communication between train drivers and the winch house on the top of the hill was a problem. The procedure adopted by the S&DR for the inclines at Brusselton and Etherley was that wagons would be aggregated at the bottom of the hill to respond to a signal from the railwayman responsible for them to indicate his wagons were ready for hauling up. At this point, a primitive signal was switched to the 'go' position. This consisted of just a white disc on a pole, turned edge on to the incline until the wagons had been correctly coupled to the ropes, when the pole would be rotated to face the engine-house. This was fine in theory but unfortunately, at Brusselton in particular, the signal was too far away from the winchman at the top of the hill to see which way the signal had been set. The pragmatic solution the company adopted, which impressed the visiting engineers, was to have a mounted telescope in the engine-house window purely for the use of the winchman. It remains to be seen what method was employed on foggy days.

Once they had completed their stint in Britain, the two engineers returned home where they went on to enjoy long and distinguished careers: Karl von Oeynhausen became the Prussian Chief Mining Councillor and later Privy Councillor in the Finance Ministry whilst Ernst von Dechen became Head of the Ministry of Mines, Factories and Salt Works and Member of the Prussian Council of State. Their report didn't get published until late in 1829, by which time steam railways in England were already proving their worth in a way the two men could barely have contemplated.

Most of the freight seen by the men visiting the S&DR was coal, but they also mention seeing coke, cinders, stone, marl, clay and ironstone, paving stones, bricks, tiles, roof slates and lime traffic.

In one of life's rich ironies, one of the company's first customers for lime transportation was Christopher Tennant. This was ironic because Tennant was the main supporter of the original canal proposal, which he had hoped would take a direct line from the south Durham coalfields to Stockton, where he lived. Tennant had vigorously opposed the detour in the proposed railway to Darlington, included purely to serve the vanities of the Darlington based proprietors. By the time the S&DR was operational, Tennant was the owner of lime kilns at nearby Thickley, just to the east of Shildon, and was magnanimously prepared to swallow his pride to ensure delivery of limestone to his kilns, and removal of lime to boats waiting at Teesside. Nevertheless, it must still have galled him that his transport costs were higher than they needed to be due to the additional time and mileage incurred by an unnecessary Darlington detour. To Tennant the solution was obvious; he had to build his own railway, and this would take the obvious direct route from coalfield to coast. The outcome was the Clarence Railway (CR), a railway created in direct competition to the S&DR, and a thorn in the side of the Darlington Quakers for many years to come.

Tennant intended to start his railway from the isolated Weardale coalfields near Willington to new docks he would create on the north bank of the Tees at Haverton Hill, five miles to the east of Stockton. In truth, the idea wasn't entirely new, there had been a similar proposal a few years earlier under the title the 'Tees and Weardale Railway', a proposal rejected by parliament in 1819. Tennant, however, made improvements to the original scheme which made it more palatable to investors. He added additional branch lines to accommodate those outlying Durham collieries currently ignored by the S&DR. At the time he came up with the proposal he was still on speaking terms with the Pease family and offered to finance his railway jointly with them, albeit using his new docks at Haverton Hill as the preferred destination. It was only when the S&DR rejected his offer he struck out on his own. On paper at least, the prospects for Tennant's railway looked good, but he soon found himself opposed by a combined force of Tyneside coal merchants and landed gentry; particularly, Lord Londonderry through whose land at Wynyard the railway had to pass. In consequence, Tennant's first Parliamentary Bill was thrown out. However, he was not easily dissuaded, and revised the proposal, this time shortening the line, such that, instead of continuing into Weardale, it terminated in central Durham. Unfortunately, this was just a few miles north of Darlington, slap-bang in the middle of S&DR territory which was a disastrous mistake to make as, initially, he had to rent operational rights over a section of the rival S&DR.

Rails were laid down linking what became Port Clarence, on the north bank of the Tees, to the S&DR at Simpasture Farm, close to where Newton Aycliffe station is today. The name 'Clarence' was chosen as a sop to the Duke of Clarence, the future William IV, who Tennant thought might be enlisted to offer royal patronage to the venture. His ploy may actually have worked because Tennant's railway bill subsequently received parliamentary approval, on 23 May 1828, after receiving a battering when previously submitted. Tennant was principal shareholder in the company, the only instance of him holding shares in any of the companies he either promoted or developed. Unfortunately, he was now in the position of siphoning trade away from the S&DR and his rival was not amused. To use their words, 'War ... open or concealed', had been declared. And if it was war it was a war the CR had little chance of winning. Tennant's problem, as noted earlier, was that during the crucial early years of its existence, the CR had to lease a few miles of S&DR rails, west of Simpasture, and despite its designation as a public railway, the S&DR made life as difficult as possible for its unwanted

Christopher Tennant.

lessee. The S&DR were even prepared to remove rails at their junction with the Clarence Railway to prevent access.[4]

A situation that began badly deteriorated further. Tennant needed finance from the principal financial institutions of the day and the Society of Friends, who owned most of the important financial institutions, closed ranks to restrict access to borrowing. This seriously delayed the completion of the CR, but worse was to follow. The moment the CR began running trains, the S&DR drastically increased charges on the short, leased section of their railway. To add insult to injury, they also insisted that CR wagons must be checked over a weighbridge before permission would be given to run over their rails while at the same time, S&DR customers' wagons only needed to be counted past the same checker. This had the anticipated effect of increasing the time taken for CR freight to get from colliery to dock, thereby obviating the shorter distance involved in using the CR as compared to the S&DR. To further pressurise their rival, the S&DR refused to allow horse-drawn CR wagons to travel over their rails during the hours of darkness, citing safety concerns, regardless of the fact that S&DR horses and those belonging to their customers were given free rein any time of day. The effect of this on CR finances was crippling and nearly succeeded in achieving the aim of bankrupting the S&DR's main opposition. As it was, the Clarence Railway survived but only began to pay shareholder dividends once the company had built their own line to central Durham via a branch from their railway at Byers Green.

Meanwhile, new coal reserves were being exploited at the western end of the S&DR. One of the company's financial backers, Jonathan Backhouse, was the part-owner of a nearby colliery. To benefit both the railway and his business, a deal was arranged whereby a new branch line would be added from his Black Boy Colliery, north of Shildon in the Dene Valley, which would connect with the S&DR, a few hundred yards east of the Mason's Arms. This was hardly straightforward since it involved laying down new rails on the steep slopes on each side of the 'Shield'. Nevertheless, the branch line, known as 'Black Boy' after that colliery, opened for business on 10 July 1827. Despite the name, 'Black Boy' has no racial overtones. It referred to the coal blackened faces of miners' children, who were often employed, as had been the young George Stephenson, doing unskilled menial work underground. Initially worked by horses, the downhill sections were controlled by 'bank-riders' who sat astride coal wagons regulating the speed of descent using crude wooden brakes.

Within a year, movement of wagons on the inclines was controlled by a new stationary engine. The new branch attracted industry and a metal foundry was soon built close by. Known as the Phoenix Foundry its proprietor was Nicholas Downing, of whom more later.

Business boomed. Towards the end of the decade, the company sought to make further appointments of senior staff to support the increasingly overworked Timothy Hackworth. An 1830 report prepared on the company's behalf by Thomas Hall of Black Boy Colliery identified where the company was vulnerable. The first appointment was Thomas MacNay. MacNay joined the company in October 1832. Initially employed on trial as a storeman, he went on to become the company's draughtsman and accountant. He remained with the company and successor organisations for the rest of his life and would be instrumental in the creation of the staff's Railway Institute. Perhaps the most important addition to staff, however, was the creation of the new role of Traffic Manager, a duty Hackworth previously tried to fit in with everything else he had to cope with day to day. The Traffic Manager became responsible for dealing with the daily scheduling and management of trains and the first to be handed the job was one of Stephenson's old Hetton Colliery colleagues, John Graham. With Graham's appointment there was now the opportunity to assess day-to-day information on what worked well and what needed changing in how the railway was organised. Graham seized the moment to take stock of both the social as well as financial implications of running a public railway in both hands.

CHAPTER THREE

Learning from mistakes

John Graham.

'Mr. Glass's son' deserves to be remembered. Why, you might ask? Well young Master Glass is the first officially recorded fatality on a public railway, even if he doesn't merit more than a passing mention in the statistics. William Huskisson MP is often wrongly quoted as being the world's first railway fatality, but his death in 1830 on the opening day of the Liverpool and Manchester Railway, albeit notorious and widely reported, followed several on the S&DR.

William Glass, whose full name only appears in a short newspaper account of his death, was by no means the first person to die on railways, not even those on the S&DR. There was, for example, the reported death of an S&DR labourer called Mossom in 1822 who, according to the company, was killed by a fall of earth during railway construction a few months prior to the opening of the railway, Mossom's widow being awarded £5 by the company and his funeral expenses paid. Nevertheless, Mr. Glass's son is the first name to feature in published national railway fatality stats.

The date when he died is stated as '30 June 1826 and the place he died 'Etherley'. So, young William Glass died on the railway close to its starting point, Witton Park Colliery.[5] He was only 15 years old at the time and the younger brother of John Glass, a loyal servant of the S&DR throughout his long working life. The date the company provided to the government as the day on which young Willam Glass is said to have died must be incorrect as he was actually buried on 25 June, so he presumably died sometime before then. Certainly not on 30 June.

The key word in the minimalist S&DR accident report here is 'recorded'. There had been deaths on the S&DR long before 1826 but none found their way into company records because the casualties involved were 'only' navvies, employed by contractors working for the S&DR during railway construction, for example, there is the record of a Thomas Lamb who was killed on 21 February

1824, being crushed beneath an embankment slump during the construction of the Brusselton incline.

By the standards of the day, these people were unaccountable. 'Mr. Glass's son', who isn't even provided with a Christian name in the report, might have been forgotten were it not for a request for a summary of railway accident statistics issued by the Board of Trade in 1839. This amounted to a retrospective of just the known *fatalities* on the Railway since 1825; not every accident involving injuries to staff or the public. The task of collating the information, such as it was, fell to the Earl of March to whom all authorised railway companies were required by parliament to respond. Being the oldest conventional railway, the S&DR had most years to consider, yet when the return from the S&DR finally dropped on Earl March's desk, the response was perfunctory at best. It contained only the barest of explanations as to how and where the casualties came to a sticky end. No information was provided on anyone who survived to tell the tale, regardless of the seriousness of their injury. In the case of Mr. Glass's son, the S&DR report on his death is short and to the point:

> **Name** 'Glass'**, location** 'Etherley'**, date** '1826 June 30'**, by what means** 'by wgs near Etherley', **comments** 'Mr. Glass's son.'

His brother John Glass was an S&DR employee, still working for the company 20 years after this incident, and this may account for the odd familiarity in the boy's description. In respect of the wording in the report the words actually say 'by do' (i.e. ditto). There are lots of similar abbreviations, the log entry quoted, for example, cites the cause of death as 'by wgs' rather than by wagons. In a separate note on the files there is an additional clue as to the cause of death namely the words 'riding-walking-playing'. It therefore appears William Glass was walking on the line at the time he was killed. There is no indication if William Glass was actually an employee at the time of the company, like his brother, although in all probability he was.

In fairness to the S&DR, since there was no legal requirement to do so, it was not normal practice, as late as 1840, for railways to keep a formal record of accidents; indeed the S&DR may be considered pioneers in this respect in that their Traffic Superintendent was logging life-threatening incidents more or less on appointment in 1831, although this may have had more to do with the adverse effect the accident had on the day-to-day running of the railway than on any consequence to the victim.

Nevertheless, the fact that only the barest information was available, when it came to the Board of Trade request, is apparent from the initial reply to Earl March's request for information, when the company's proprietor Joseph Pease could only promise:

'to provide the best list that can be obtained of accidents on the railway which have proved fatal' by going 'carefully through the police reports and committee books since the railway opened in 1825.'

The result, which looks to have been compiled from odd notes and scraps of paper sitting around in company files, was just a list of deaths assembled in non-chronological order, with most of the relevant detail missing. The record is far from complete as even the most cursory investigation of stories in the *Durham County Advertiser* show, e.g. there was the death on the S&DR of a foundry man, William Barkas, in November 1836. There is also a letter on the company's file showing coroner's fees paid in respect of four other deaths, in 1835 and 1836, whose names don't appear in the 1839 report. There is also undated correspondence from the same time on deaths not otherwise recorded.

Since the date of the incident is often missing from the company record, this raises the intriguing possibility that at least some of these tragedies predate that of William Glass. The off-hand low-key manner in which the deaths were recorded is an indication of how cheap human life was at that time. Many of the people killed on the railway are not even given a name; there is just a space where the name should be with a few words saying how they died; e.g. 'killed near Newport by wagon wheels', 'killed by an engine whilst crossing Thornaby Lane', 'killed by a coal wagon at Stockton', etc. Sadly, but perhaps unsurprisingly, at least 10 per cent of the fatalities involved children straying on to the line. The death at Thornaby Lane, cited above, is ascribed to 'boy waiting for the coach to Darlington', whilst the following entry refers to 'child' with no further expansion as to how the unfortunate infant met its end. Railways, it is true, were beyond the experience of the general public at the time and their risks barely understood. Typical of the infant tragedies is that of Mary Robson, aged 11, who went into the 'engine house' close to her home on 28 February 1845, where there was a tap that offered both the convenience and luxury of fresh water. As she was filling the family's 'water tin' she was struck by the tender of a reversing engine which ran over her, badly crushing her left leg, an injury from which she later died. The S&DR concluded that, since she was obviously trespassing, it had no responsibility for her death and no further action was taken.

Correspondence to the railway committee at New Shildon in the thirties and forties suggests that hair-raising incidents involving children were commonplace and perhaps the most poignant concerned the fate of the Lister family. William Lister was an employee of the S&DR and on one devastating day in 1837 Lister's wife and only child were killed. All we know about this incident, from company records, is that the family members were 'run over by loaded wagons' at the company's Darlington depot. On the face of it this seems astonishing. What were they all doing wandering around the busy depot unchallenged at the same time? The thought, therefore, occurs that they may have been waiting for William Lister snr. to finish his shift. If so, the poor man may have been one of the first on the scene and, worse still, even witnessed the event? It's probably better in this instance not to know the full story. Lister was especially unfortunate in respect of railway accidents. Two men, described in successive entries as 'relation to Mr. Lister', were killed by a 'merchandise train' and 'coal wagons' at Darlington and Stockton respectively in 1839.

Accidents caused by mechanical failures of engines or rolling stock were, surprisingly, less common than those attributable to human error. Right from the start, it was more likely that someone would fall under the wheels of a shunting wagon than be injured due to some inadequacy in loco mechanics. Indeed, as noted earlier, there were two such incidents on the opening day (27 September 1825). The first involving a man who 'received a severe blow' when struck by a shunting wagon and the second concerning a man called John Stevens, who when clinging to the outside of the solitary passenger coach fell under the wheels, and whose leg was so badly crushed it led to immediate amputation. Given the primitive nature of medical expertise at the time, this almost certainly resulted in his death.

Unfortunately, accidents involving people being run down by steam engines are much harder to identify prior to 1825 as they are subsumed into more general statistics on industrial fatalities (particularly those that occurred at collieries), which were regular events. So, it is only with the advent of public railways using steam locomotives, of which the S&DR was the first, that there is an expectation that the welfare of the wider population need be taken into consideration. Health and safety, in terms of both company employees and the public at large, was initially a matter of trial and error. The fact is there was no precedent. As noted earlier, members of the public were originally allowed to hitch a free ride on any passing wagon, a disastrous practice which, if not condoned, was largely ignored by the management. Accidents involving people illicitly riding in wagons occurred so often on the S&DR that the company felt obliged to place an advert in the 16 March 1832 edition of the *Durham County Advertiser*:

> 'in consequence of serious accidents … men would be stationed at intervals along the line to provide information of any Person or Persons who shall be found riding upon a locomotive engine, wagon or other carriage not duly licensed to carry passengers.'

Whose 'wagons' were 'duly licensed' to carry passengers isn't clear and no details of the 'serious accidents' referred to in the advertisement made it through to the 1839 Board of Trade statistics.

Accidents involving the company's own employees were considered an acceptable hazard that went with the job. It was practice, for example, in the first twenty years, for S&DR drivers and firemen to carry out oiling and greasing of rolling stock wheels whilst the train was on the move. To avoid unnecessary delay, footplatemen waited until their train had started a moderate descent and then stepped down from the engine to stand either side of the moving train applying oil to the wheels as each wagon passed by. Often the additional lubrication was sufficient alone to cause an increase in train speed. This required the footplatemen to leap aboard a tail-end truck and make their way back to the cab clambering from wagon to wagon over stacked heaps of coal. One unfortunate driver called Joseph Musgrove paid the ultimate price for this. Whilst trying to apply grease to carriage wheels, on some unspecified date at West Hartburn (near Stockton), he fell between two wagons and was 'run over'. Given the hazardous nature of this enterprise the only surprise is that Musgrove is the only such recorded death in Graham's reports.

Although you were more likely to die under the wheels of a moving train, accidents resulting from engine failures, as was the case on colliery railways, were also regular events. Perhaps the most widely reported was the boiler explosion of *Locomotion No.1*

on 4 July 1828 at Heighington, which killed driver John Cree, and seriously injured fireman Edward Turnbull. Cree had been married barely two months on the day he died.

According to the S&DR response to the Board of Trade, the boiler exploded 'owing to his (Cree's) negligence'. What negligence was involved in poor Cree's demise is not expanded upon, but the root cause of this and other similar accidents was well understood. It had become common practice to hold down the engine's primitive safety valve, essentially a weighted plug in the top of the boiler, to increase steam pressure whenever the engine appeared to be a bit sluggish. The company was well aware of this and turned a blind eye for the sake of expediency. In fact, Cree is almost certainly not the first person on the S&DR to lose his life in this way. Earlier, another engineman, whose name isn't recorded, was on the footplate of the S&DR engine No.5 *Stockton* near Simpasture when the boiler exploded. Unfortunately, there are no details of how the incident occurred since the report of the man's death didn't make it through to the 1839 stats. Hewison's book *Locomotive Boiler*

Stephenson's *Locomotion No.1* at Darlington's Head of Steam museum.

Explosions gives the date as 19 March 1828. However, the *British Locomotive Catalogue* states the explosion occurred in October 1826, which fits better with the known S&DR locomotive chronology and would also explain why the 1828, *Locomotion* explosion, was recorded but the *Stockton* explosion wasn't.

The company rarely, if at all, admitted liability and, by absolving itself of blame, learnt nothing from the men's deaths. The outcome was, that just one year after the *Locomotion* explosion, a driver called Gillespie died in an almost identical incident when the same unhappy engine burst its boiler once more. If the explosion only caused injuries, such as when Hackworth's passenger engine *Globe* blew up at Middlesbrough Station in January 1837, the company was more concerned about the cost of the engine than the safety of the public or their own staff. *Locomotion* wasn't the unluckiest engine, however, in the New Shildon stable in terms of fatal accidents. There was an engine called *Adelaide*, which, in the space of a few weeks mowed down and killed three men in separate incidents. Two were contractors working trackside and the third is just described as a 'traveller'. The comments column next to the fatality report, unusually for the S&DR, expands on how one of the men was killed. He had apparently tried to cross the line to light his pipe from the fire in the grate of the engine *Wilberforce* when he met his end. Even in those far-off days it seems smoking wasn't good for your health.

Railway crossings were sufficiently novel as to be regular sources of accidents. Nowadays, we associate steam locomotives with the distinctive sound of their whistles. As late as 1831, whistles were still not being fitted to S&DR engines. Instead, footplatemen were expected to ring a hand-bell when approaching road crossings, or when they saw people working next to the track.[6] On 19 October 1839, Thomas Grey and a man called Fowlis were killed, along with the three horses they were escorting over a crossing at Guisborough Lane, by a train fronted by *Raby Castle*. This is the only incident which seems to have cost the S&DR a significant amount in compensation (£1,400), although whether this was paid to victims' families or was merely the legal fees paid for the train's 'conductor', Appleton, against whom a private prosecution had been brought, isn't clear. In the event, the jury threw out the separate prosecution case. Amongst other fatal casualties that year was a certain Robert Stephenson, perhaps one of George Stephenson's many relatives, which included his brother James (or 'Jem'), who worked for the

S&DR. This could explain why his departure is permitted more than the usual couple of words of explanation, although the reporter's command of English is questionable:

> 'Run over by a stone wagon which was going to be left by a train drawn by an engine on which he was riding and had left off on front to catch the forward train beside.'

The last entry in the Board of Trade accident report dates from December 1839 and relates to a publican called Phillips from Yarm who was knocked down and killed whilst trespassing, whilst drunk, on the railway at Urlay Nook.

The above details, however, hardly provide a complete picture of even the fatal accidents on the S&DR. Some of those originally identified by the company for inclusion in the parliamentary report never made it to Westminster, or at least were so understated as to be rendered invisible. These include the story of an old 'match' woman caught 'walking on the way' and run over by the engine *Darlington* at a location described as 'below old river bridge' and a blind woman and her dog killed whilst crossing the rails at Yarm Lane. There is also an undated report of a 'tinker' killed by 'two engines' whilst 'coming along the line'. How the tinker came to be killed by *two* engines unfortunately isn't explained. More understandably omitted is the demise of a train passenger called Gerrard who, when travelling between Stockton and Darlington, 'made too free with a cask of spirits which was also for Darlington. It is supposed the spirits killed him'. What a way to go!

Drunkenness, as today, was a common cause of accidents. In March 1841, John Garbutt fell asleep alongside the track whilst 'intoxicated' at Stockton. Garbutt unfortunately left his hand on the rails and found it missing when he woke up. A few weeks later, a man called Gillespie was even more unfortunate when he attempted to sleep off a surfeit of drink using the rails as a pillow.

An obvious source of concern was rope-worked inclines. The first official death on an incline was at Brusselton. In February 1831 Thomas Johnson was killed by a 'wagon'. There is no other detail on how this happened, but the chances are that Johnson was illegally riding a waggon up the incline when he slipped and fell beneath the wheels since such incidents feature regularly in Board of Trade accident reports.

Having walked up Brusselton incline myself, I can tell you the opportunity of hitching a ride to the summit must have been very tempting. Although there are vague references to non-fatal accidents involving people illegally riding the inclines, it was another 11 years before a boy called Thomas Robertson, employed by West Auckland Colliery, was killed on one. On this occasion, he was working near the foot of Brusselton incline and was attempting to reverse a horse and wagons into a siding when his foot got trapped in a crossover rail. How long he was there before he was struck by a loaded coal wagon travelling down the incline isn't known but it seems probable he had plenty of time to contemplate his fate before the fatal impact. Typical of the value of human life at the time, in one of the earliest awards made by the government against a railway company, is the case of West Auckland Colliery that was awarded compensation for 'damage to the horse and one of their wagons'. People injured on railways were, apparently, worth less than property and sometimes the only recourse for compensation for the families of a victim was to go cap-in-hand and appeal to the generosity of the railway. There are dozens of such letters in the archives at Kew, with perhaps the most poignant dating from June 1845:

'I trust you will excuse the liberty caused by an accident and dire necessity. My husband lately died in a lunatic asylum leaving me with five children entirely depending upon me for support. On the 1st Inst. one of my daughters (aged 12) while employed in carrying milk and crossing your railroad, near Bowerfield Lane (*probably Bowesfield Lane*), Stockton, was accidentally knocked down by a railway wagon then passing (without blame attaching to anyone) from which her right arm had to be amputated close by the shoulder and was otherwise much bruised, particularly her right leg. By this accident and having to devote most of my attention to her, attended with considerable expense and loss of enumeration for labour I had previously been employed in, and my only pecuniary assistance at present arising from parochial relief, being entirely inadequate to supply even the common necessities of life compel me most humbly and respectfully to request you to take my distressing case before the committee.'

It is unlikely that the (alleged) author, Martha Swan, probably the 'laundress' Martha Swan, a resident of Stockton according to the 1841 census whose daughter's name was also Martha, was literate.

One thing for sure, no labourer's wife would use words such as 'pecuniary' and 'enumeration'. The inclusion of the word 'parochial' suggests the letter was perhaps written on her behalf by her local clergyman. Further correspondence with the S&DR took place in which Martha Swan confirmed her daughter 'remains a cripple' so the child's leg must have been more badly damaged than first appeared. The elaborate wording of her appeal seems to have helped her case as the committee were moved to make a small award, but what this amounted to isn't recorded.

From 1 January 1840, records of all accidents, and not just fatalities, were formally maintained and one of the first, which occurred on the S&DR (1 July 1840), concerned a 'deaf and dumb travelling fortune teller' who, while trespassing on the railway, was knocked down by a wagon which crushed his leg. In this instance it is said he recovered from the injury but doubtless his failure to foresee the event would have seriously damaged his professional credibility. After 1840, more detail appears in the incident reports and these provide additional background to the recorded event. The death of a 15-year-old youth called Thomas Maunsey is extensively reported. Employed by the South Durham Colliery, he was proceeding to work 'on the tender of the *Prince* engine' when, close to the South Durham Branch of the Bishop Auckland and Weardale Railway, 'he wilfully jumped off and fell in front of the tender wheel which passed over his left groin and crushed him'. He was taken to the Mason's Arms, the acting admin office of the S&DR in New Shildon, where he died three hours later. What poor Thomas was doing 'on the tender', which seems to have been part of his recognised duties, isn't indicated and the word 'wilfully' isn't used much today in respect of someone's accidental death. How the company determined that Maunsey's action was 'wilful' also isn't recorded but there is, once again, more than a hint of self-righteousness in the company's summary of events.

So much for the fatalities. There is insufficient detail in the Board of Trade report to identify cause and effect, so it is fortunate that John Graham kept a journal of dangerous incidents on the S&DR, whether they resulted in injury or not. These provide a fascinating portrait of the evolution of safe railway practice. Amongst the fascinating, if disturbing, incidents reported are those relating to the use of 'dandy carts'.

As noted, until the 1850s, mineral traffic on the S&DR comprised an odd assortment of steam and horse drawn trains, with the latter

Horse drawn
trains (from a
nineteenth century
engraving).

dominated by private operators employing a horse and three or
four wagons. Better used to driving carts on turnpike roads, the
drivers were a law unto themselves. Let loose on a public railway
their dangerously wayward practises were largely ignored until
some incident occurred that directly threatened company finances.
On downhill sections of the line, which effectively meant most of
the railway between colliery and coast, no motive power apart from
gravity was deemed necessary. At such times, the horse trotted
alongside the train while the wagons freewheeled, with the driver
astride the buffers of the primitive braking wagon. This was a waste of
the horse's energy and George Stephenson recommended the company
use a low-sided open-backed dandy cart attached to the rear of the
train, where the horse could take a well-earned rest if not required.
The origin of the term 'dandy' in this context isn't clear although in
Victorian times 'dandy' apparently was applied to anything new or
innovative and was used liberally in non-railway contexts, as in the
expression 'fine and dandy' or as a man devoted to fashion and style.
Its nearest modern equivalent is 'cool'. The invention of the dandy cart
is attributed to various people, including Stephenson and Timothy
Hackworth, but dandy carts were common on the continent at this
time, so the jury is out on where they actually originated.

Most depictions of dandy carts, e.g. the illustration in Tomlinson's
book about the NER and the example at the NRM at York, show
the horse standing. In truth this was virtually impossible for the
horse if the train was moving. Horses therefore sat back on their
haunches, as dogs do. Horses became so familiar with this principle
that, as Tomlinson reports, if the cart wasn't attached to the train an
untethered horse would attempt to climb into the end wagon. It is

interesting that the death of horses belonging to their customers was usually costlier to the railway company than the death of their own personnel. Until the creation of a mutual insurance scheme in the 1840s railway families had little recourse if the main breadwinner was killed or seriously injured during the tenure of his employment.

The dandy cart procedure involved unhitching the horse on the crest of a hill, where it waited as the wagons rolled slowly by. The horse leapt aboard as the dandy cart passed. A bale of hay was kept in the cart to encourage the horse in this, but in fact the opportunity for a nice rest was all the incentive the horses needed. It is interesting that the death of horses belonging to their customers was invariably costlier to the railway company than the death of any of their staff.

The dandy cart concept was reasonable for trains whose top speed rarely exceeded 5mph. Problems only arose because of wide variability in dandy cart management. In the months following his appointment as Traffic Manager, John Graham received reports of several incidents where practice fell greatly short of expectations. On 4 August 1831, for example, Thomas Sanderson, an 'independent' driver, who enjoyed the odd drink, climbed into the dandy cart to sleep off a lunchtime skin-full leaving his horse free to labour uphill unsupervised, drawing a half-dozen loaded wagons. The steep slope took its toll and the wagons to a crawl. Following on behind was a train headed by the engine *Globe*, which duly collided with the rear of the horse-drawn coal wagons, derailing *Globe* and blocking the line for two hours (and no doubt seriously disturbing Sanderson's beauty sleep). The driver's ill-judged nap cost him a 5/- fine from the S&DR.

On 24 November that same year, there were two further incidents involving dandy carts. In the first, driver Thomas Leng failed to slow his wagons sufficiently on the descent at Myers Flat. The intention had been to aggregate his wagons to the train ahead, but he lost control of them and they careered down the hill to collide with the dandy cart of the train in front. The collision ejected the resident horse, which was hurled down the adjacent embankment. Leng was fined 2/6. There is no record of what happened to the horse. Later that same day, driver George Snaith, in an almost identical incident, failed to keep control of his wagons on the long downward run into Darlington. The trucks caught up with the train in front and collided with the dandy cart, this time not only despatching the horse onto the trackside but also Snaith himself. The horse emerged unhurt, but deserved retribution was enacted on Snaith who broke his leg and was fined 5 shillings for his troubles.

It has been noted elsewhere that the residents of Central Durham, and particularly the population of New Shildon, liked the occasional tipple. In consequence, alcohol was often a contributory, if not the

S&DR dandy cart
at the NRM, York.

major, factor in many of the hair-raising incidents on the S&DR. In 1832, driver William Ogle and his number two, George Hodgson, staggered bleary-eyed from a Shildon alehouse to take charge of a horse-drawn coal train. Shortly after setting off, indeed on the first downhill section, their dandy cart parted company with the rails. Neither Ogle the driver nor his equally sozzled cohort, who was the nominal brakeman, noticed that the cart was now bouncing along behind tearing up the track. Oblivious to the carnage being caused, and inflamed by drink, Ogle ignored warnings from trackside and refused to give way to anyone in his path. An oncoming horse-drawn train was obliged to reverse and take refuge in the first available siding despite having right-of-way. When Ogle came face to face with a steam hauled coal train headed by the Stephenson designed engine *William IV*, he refused to give way and let it pass, as required by company rules. A pitched battle ensued, involving both drivers, to which Ogle's drunken colleague Hodgson enthusiastically contributed. The brawl spread to the footplate of *William IV*, where Ogle was eventually overcome by his sober opposition. This was not the end of the confrontation, however, Ogle it seems was a sore loser. Before the *William IV* had chance to move away Ogle tried to derail it by placing a rail and supporting chair on the track in front of it. All these escapades were too much even for the normally laissez-faire S&DR, and Ogle and Hodgson were referred to a local magistrate for prosecution.

Beer-fuelled belligerence seems to have been a regular event. A couple of months earlier, Robert Sanderson, William Vasey and Michael Howe abandoned their train to pursue thirst-quenching activities at a pub in Spring Gardens, effectively blocking all subsequent traffic movement on the main line. They were all fined 2/6. Driving a train must have been a thirsty business since Sanderson and his mates were not the only railwaymen who chose to take on liquid refreshment at inappropriate moments. Rather than complete their coal delivery to a waiting collier-boat at Newport, near Middlesbrough, eight railwaymen deserted the wagons and disappeared into a pub for several hours, preventing the ship they were supposed to be loading from departing. They were fined 10 shillings. In that instance, Sanderson and associates were not employed directly by the S&DR, but this type of behaviour wasn't confined to non-company drivers. John Lydle, for example, an S&DR driver, was reported to the railway committee in July 1833 for leaving his locomotive at Heighington station after sinking one too many at a nearby alehouse. His train had to be moved to its destination, Stockton, by two firemen. Rather than receiving plaudits for his commendable reluctance to drive whilst under the influence, his employers took a dim view and Lydle was dismissed.

Single line working was another factor which caused conflict. Independent operators saw no reason to concede ground to anyone else, and, particularly, if so required by paid employees of the S&DR. This was a problem since at the beginning the railway was mostly single line interspersed with passing places. Typical of the problems raised was an incident involving drivers William Myers and John Pears, nominally in charge of a horse and four wagons, who refused to pull over to allow a steam train to pass. Oblivious to the abuse hurled at them, they prevented the train behind from passing for more than 4 miles. They were each fined 5/-. On stretches of single line, in the absence of signals, the S&DR installed marker posts at fixed intervals trackside. The posts divided the track into sections of varying length, the distance between them defined by assumed driver visibility. Right of way was allotted to the first train to pass one of the posts and thereby enter a designated section. Once the train had claimed right of way, trains travelling in the opposite direction were expected to reverse into the nearest passing loop and permit their opposite number to pass. This, however, was rag-to-bull provocation for the independent hauliers. Ralph Hall, with a horse drawn train, despite seeing that an oncoming train had beaten him past a section marker, refused to give way, resulting in a stand-off between the drivers closely followed by fisticuffs. In Hall's case this was the latest in a series of similar brawls and his access to the Railway was withdrawn.

Although officially forbidden, members of the public often rode on the driver's platform with footplatemen or were allowed, subject to some back-pocket contribution, to ride on top of loaded coal wagons. Engine drivers, who were self-employed in the early years, treated trains as their private taxi service. Typical of this was an occasion in November 1831, when S&DR driver Ed Corner was fined 2/6 for allowing a man and a woman who Corner had only just met to travel with him on the footplate, subject to some unrecorded backhand payment, This was a repetition of something for which he had only recently received an official warning.

In recounting these workforce misdemeanours, it is only fair to say that the railway company itself was hardly a paragon when it came to safe working practices. Two of their apprentices needed to have limbs amputated following avoidable shunting accidents

The potential hazards associated with illegal footplate rides are well illustrated in this picture of the Hackworth designed locomotive *Middlesbrough*. The fireman is shown alongside the driver. Normally he would have been at the other end of the boiler feeding coal into the firebox, shown to the left of the chimney, from a separate tender (picture courtesy Jane Hackworth-Young).

in 1835. George Graham, the son of the Traffic Manager and then a company driver, personally witnessed failures in equipment and work procedures which resulted in accidents and 'near misses'. Some of these resulted from the fact that none of the early S&DR locomotives were provided with brakes. Stopping an engine meant separating the gears from the engine drive and then turning a handle rapidly to switch the gear into reverse. On a falling gradient this was difficult, since it involved turning the wheel in the opposite direction to that of the engine's wheels at the rate of four turns of the handle for every wheel revolution. This was nearly impossible after dark since the driver and fireman couldn't see the engine's wheels, and lamps were not routinely carried on the footplate. In fact, the company issued an instruction as early as 1831 about providing lighting to identify the presence of trains but the wording was sufficiently ambiguous as to be meaningless. It read:

> 'All engine-men, coach and wagon drivers to carry good and sufficient lights, affixed in conspicuous parts of their train, in conformity with the company's by-laws.'

In consequence, John Usher's horse drawn train on the section between Eaglescliffe and Darlington was hit from behind by another train fronted by *Rocket*, not in fact Robert Stephenson's famous *Rocket* from the Rainhill trials but another engine of the same name, a collision which killed Usher's horse. It transpired that both trains had been invisible to each other right up to the moment of impact. Compensation paid by the S&DR for injuries to horses belonging to their customers invariably exceeded that paid to the families of their own injured railwaymen. This led to the creation of Mutual Societies which provided financial support in such cases.

The outcome of this incident was, that when driving at night, footplatemen were required to carry lengths of tarry rope which were lit and hung from the outside of the boiler to alert other trains of their approach.

Engine breakdown was a daily occurrence on the S&DR into the 1850s and beyond, and the methods employed for dealing with them were often horrendous. One wet November afternoon, George Graham, working without a fireman, a practice officially frowned upon but nevertheless commonplace, was despatched from Shildon with a relief engine for a passenger train whose locomotive had broken down between Middlesbrough and Redcar. Parts of the engine had seized due to sand blowing on to the track from the banks of the Tees. After exchanging locos, Graham was to deliver the defective engine back to Shildon for repair. Unfortunately, it was barely operational. Graham nevertheless gamely set off back with it, stopping every couple of miles to crawl underneath and apply oil to the wheels and moving parts to keep the locomotive moving. It transpired that the previous driver had also used salt instead of fresh water in the boiler. This led to surging and continual ejection of boiler water from the chimney. The surging unfortunately also meant that the water-level gauge on the engine was of little practical use. Graham, therefore, had to stop every mile to make some crude estimate of how much water he still had left. During one such stop near Darlington, Graham was approached by a stranded workmate who asked for a lift back to Shildon. It wasn't long after the engine restarted before the hitchhiker began to regret his request. Over the following miles, punctuated by stops and starts for oil and water checks and with water jetting out of the chimney, he became so worried for his life he asked to jump ship despite being miles from his destination. He told Graham it was safer walking in the dark during heavy rain than run the risk of being blown up.

It was not uncommon for railwaymen to work long hours. By 1844, albeit less than 20 years since the S&DR opened for business, the S&DR was now just one small part of a national railway network. In October of that year, George Graham and George Scott (an Outside Locomotive Foreman) were sent by William Bouch, the Chief Engineer at New Shildon, to collect four engines the company had bought from the Midland Railway (MR) at Derby. The two men were put up overnight in a hotel and, being strange to the bed, Graham found he couldn't sleep. The locos were not ready for collection the following day and, during that evening, there was a dance at the inn which kept Graham awake all night. Consequently, it wasn't until 2.30am on the third day, by which time Graham had been awake for nearly 70 hours, that the two men were told the engines were ready to be taken away. They hooked up the engines, with one in steam pulling the other three, and started the long haul back to Shildon. By now it was 4am. For the first few miles of the journey the Shildon men were supported by a local 'conductor' who was supposed to travel with them to show them the way, at least until it got light, since neither Graham nor Scott had worked the line before. Unfortunately, their conductor could only be persuaded to stay with them as far as Clay Cross where he jumped ship. It was still dark and, in Graham's words, 'We did not know one yard of the line, or any signals between Clay Cross and Darlington.' Graham was at the controls and Scott was firing. The engine itself was in a bad way, leaking water and losing boiler pressure. At Altofts Junction, where the lines from Derby to Leeds and York separated, the Shildon men took the wrong turning and travelled several miles towards Leeds before they realised their mistake. In panic, they reversed their train of dead engines back to the junction. By now Graham could hardly keep his eyes open and later could remember nothing about the remainder of the journey. The whole trip from Derby had taken 18 hours, by which time Graham had been awake for nearly 3½ days. By some miracle they made it home. Only with the advent of trade unionism, and in the wake of several high profile serious rail accidents, would the working conditions of lower ranked railway employees improve.

It wasn't always the company's fault. Graham himself could also be dangerously maverick when the opportunity arose. On Good Friday 1861, Graham was asked by John Dixon, the S&DR Consulting Engineer, to carry out a trial to determine the friction of a newer and heavier type of coal wagon the company were thinking of investing in. The test ground was a steeply falling gradient between Barnard Castle and Darlington and the plan was to freewheel loaded trucks, without braking, down the 1/82 gradient to see if the wagons gained sufficient momentum, during the 10 miles of descent, to propel the train all the way up the rising gradient into Darlington without further need for motive power. For the experiment, eight loaded trucks and a guard's van housing 12 brave souls, recruited to measure speed and stability, optimistically took to the rails. In theory, the men in the guard's van were also present to act as emergency brakemen for the train using the crude van brake. Since this was a Bank Holiday, the line between Barnard Castle and Darlington was closed to traffic and all the level crossings between the two towns were barred to road users. Graham stationed himself at the 10-mile point, near Winston Station, to best observe proceedings first hand. It was not expected that the wagons would achieve anything near 60mph, since that was the fastest speed achievable by the express trains of the day. However, by the time the experimental rig burst through Winston station, it was already travelling at 73mph and still accelerating, with two miles of further descent remaining. From Graham's vantage point on the embankment near the station he watched in horror as the train careered round a bend towards the platform, each wagon swaying ominously, in Graham's words, 'like a duck'. The train barely slowed as it climbed out of the river valley. Meanwhile, in the guard's van, all attempts to apply the handbrake during the descent had failed and the entombed men committed their souls to God, convinced they were about to die. The speed of the uncontrolled wagons now exceeded the limit of the measurement gauges installed in the van. The situation for the men was made worse by the fact that the van's only window was obscured by dust blown off the coal wagons, leaving the 12 men awaiting their fate in almost total blackout. In the end their luck held. When the track began to level out the train slowed sufficient for the van brake to bite and the decelerating wagons were safely diverted into a siding just outside Darlington where the runaway was finally brought to a halt. A red-faced Graham reported the shambles to his manager the following day, who was, by all accounts, 'very severe on the matter' although what other outcome might have been expected given the dodgy nature of the experiment is by no means clear.

Although there were speed limits imposed by the company from the start, this didn't stop drivers using every means within their power to reduce journey-time, whilst coincidentally increasing refreshment-break-time. In 1833 a driver was reported for running a non-stop steam-hauled train from Shildon to Middlesbrough, a feat previously thought to be impossible since the locomotive had to stop to take on water at regular intervals. It transpired that the driver had an ingenious method of collecting water on the hoof. On falling gradients, as he neared the principal water stopping points at Darlington and Eaglescliffe, he uncoupled the engine and accelerated the detached loco forward to the water stop, leaving the rest of the train, now in the hands of the fireman, to freewheel slowly down the hill under gravity. Assuming the wagons slowed sufficiently, he would then move his engine away from the water tank in front of the approaching wagons. Once the speed of locomotive and wagons matched he would climb on the tender and, standing astride the buffers, couple the engine back on to the train. There is no indication in company reports that this practice ended once the company were aware of what was happening, although its presence in Graham's 'incident' journal suggests that it wasn't encouraged. The same driver regularly dropped his fireman off at Darlington (where he lived) on Saturday nights, so his pal got an early finish. He then drove and fired the engine the remaining eight miles to Shildon without assistance. Since the Hackworth designed locomotives of the time had a 'U' tube type boiler which required the presence of a driver at one end of the engine and a fireman at the other it is by no means clear how this was done, but it would no doubt once again have involved some further acrobatics.

In truth, positive innovation such as this was neither likely nor expected from a workforce composed, at least at first, of unskilled men drawn from mainly agricultural stock. Since railways paid better than farm work there was a huge demand for jobs. In the period 1830 to 1840, the S&DR was inundated with requests for work from vagrants, described by the Traffic Manager as being 'of weak intellect' who, being unable to gain employment elsewhere, were after unskilled work. Like illegal immigrants today, these men gathered together in informal camps close to the company's headquarters at New Shildon, sleeping rough or utilising the trackside equipment storage cabins. On one occasion, rather than offend these transients unnecessarily, John Graham told a delegation who presented themselves at his office that he couldn't take them on as they didn't own their own watches, which he assured them were essential tools for professional railwaymen. The following month the same men appeared again, this time brandishing watches, acquired presumably from the less security conscious townspeople, who would doubtless be arriving late for work or missing crucial appointments from then on. The deficiencies of low-paid employees were often cited by skilled railwaymen as a reasonable excuse for bad practice. Driver Robert Pickering, summoned before the S&DR board following a series of misdemeanours, blamed all his misdemeanours on a succession of 'unsatisfactory' firemen he had been allocated. When asked to name them, however, he could only recall their nicknames, 'Badger', 'Bullet', 'Baggy' and 'Buck'. Unimpressed by the defence offered, Pickering was given his marching orders.

The upper echelons of management were equally culpable in terms of unsafe working practices. The top men considered the railway their personal plaything, effectively a giant train set which could be let out to others at the management's discretion. In 1838, the S&DR applied to the Clarence Railway (CR) for permission to run passenger trains on their rails. A meeting was arranged with the CR's General Manager, Mr. Child which was attended by George Stephenson and John Graham. Child invited Stephenson and Graham to breakfast. He lived just outside Stockton and arranged for their train to stop right outside his lineside home. While the passengers on the train sat and fumed, Child and his invited guests sat down and ate a hearty breakfast, resuming their journey only after they had finished their meal.

If later railway companies learned from mistakes and changed working procedures the S&DR, being the first in the field, was reluctant to discard tried and trusted practices established on inception regardless of whether technology or general railway safety practice had moved on. Horses, for example, continued to be used on the S&DR long after they had been replaced by locos on other railways. Although the company made representations to their customers to deter them from using their own drivers and wagons – even offering financial incentives to do so – horses continued to plod along certain S&DR rails well beyond the company's incorporation into the North Eastern Railway. This practice might well have had something to do with the S&DR's insistence that the Clarence Railway only use horses and not locomotives on the section of the S&DR line the CR leased. Dandy carts too, survived until 1856 and modern signalling did not appear until well after the NER took charge. The S&DR experimented with surrogate methods, including the dubious use of putting a lighted candle in a Station Master's window, to indicate to approaching trains that the road ahead was clear. Part of the problem at the S&DR, in respect of enforcing health and safety, was the 'men's club' atmosphere built up over many years, since everyone in the company knew everyone else and no-one wanted to tell tales on friends or colleagues. Things got better under the auspices of the North Eastern Railway, as staff management, signalling, braking and rolling stock quality improved. Following government intervention, locomotive maintenance also got better as the century wore on. The last recorded boiler explosion involving a Shildon engine occurred on 17 July 1888, when locomotive 590 detonated near Simpasture. It is a measure of how much engine construction had improved since the bad old days, however, that the men on the footplate now had a solid metal cabin around them as protection and, unlike *Locomotion's* driver John Cree, the crew, despite being badly scalded, lived to tell the tale.[7]

CHAPTER FOUR

Shildon's locomotives and engine sheds

Shildon engine shed as it appeared shortly before closure.

The North Eastern Railway Company (NER) issued a specification for the rebuilding of 'engine stables' at New Shildon in July 1886, inviting tenders for the reconstruction work. That the buildings were still referred to as stables suggests that locomotives continued to be viewed as mechanical horses, at least in some quarters. The 'stables' in question consisted of two roundhouses arranged in series and although major rebuild work would be involved, the tender neither invited nor expected the demolition and replacement of existing structures. Rather, this work would extend and upgrade the buildings already there. Thus, the original roundhouse, shown as 'Sebastopol' on early site plans, was retained and increased in size. The bill of quantities included: removal of the two outer circular walls; replacement of roof and support columns; widening of the existing turntables; extensions of the engine pits;

and the installation of modern gas lighting plus improved drainage. An additional turntable was also to be added, immediately west of the others and all three were to be enclosed within a brick-built longhouse. Everything that could be recovered from the original roundhouses was to be retained for future use. As with earlier shed reconstructions, involving both the S&DR and NER, the 1886 project built on what was already there. From the first days of operation, changes to the railway site had been gradual. Shildon Works itself had grown up around the original four cottages built before the first train left for Stockton.

The origin of the Works and 'stables' can be traced to a brief note in a committee report dating from July 1825, two months before the railway officially opened. The resident engineer, Thomas Storey, was told:

> 'it was highly desirable that carpenters and blacksmiths shops be erected at the east end of the Brusselton Inclined plane…. [and that] … Thos Storey be directed to produce a design of such shops.'[8]

From such humble beginnings, the world's first public railway steam locomotive maintenance and manufacturing works came into being, with the original 2-track engine shed just a crude open sided barn accommodating two engines. Robert Young wrote that there was also, initially, no roof on the shed either, which begs the question as to what was actually there.

No plans have survived of that building, but, despite a note in the *British Shed Directory* that it was 'somewhere in the vicinity of Shildon station', it remains a reasonable assumption it was close to the engine sheds that eventually replaced it, since they were at the foot of Brusselton incline where the rest of the railway support infrastructure was located.[9] The original open-sided building must have been a bleak place in winter, barely the equivalent of a carport, and in the first five years of the railway's existence it changed little. Even the horses that continued to work the railway seem to have been provided with better accommodation in brick-built stables that survived to the end of the Second World War. For the first year, the engine shed was open to the elements; Stephenson wrote to Hackworth in December, 'I hope by this time you have got the shops covered in; so as to get the Engines under cover to repair them'. A roof didn't appear until 1826. There is a description of the original fixtures and fittings of the 'works' in the Shildon Railway Institute centenary report of 1933:

> 'There were only hand lathes on the premises, there was no turntable, no means of raising heavy parts but by ropes and pulleys, and no appliance for lifting engines or boilers but the screw jack of ancient design with four 'horns', to which a lever was attached to work the jack. Boilers and cylinders were obtained from Newcastle and wheels - then of metal and only lasting a month - procured from Bradford and other towns.'

Plans were drawn up in 1838 for a more substantial shed, 'near the watering station at Shildon', suggesting it was close to the site of the current railway station, but whether this is the case and what exactly this shed amounted to is unclear. All we know for certain is that the contract for its construction was given to George Harker, and the total cost of the work was £88 15/-. This minimal outlay suggests the building was somewhat limited in scale. Another shed was added nearby in 1842, this time significantly bigger judging by the increase in cost to £300, although there is almost no information about its construction either. It was certainly built, because there are company reports that the roof was modified the following year to allow for the installation of cowls to remove engine smoke. During the 1830s there

Plan of Shildon Works as it was in the 1850's (reproduced from the 1855 O.S. map).

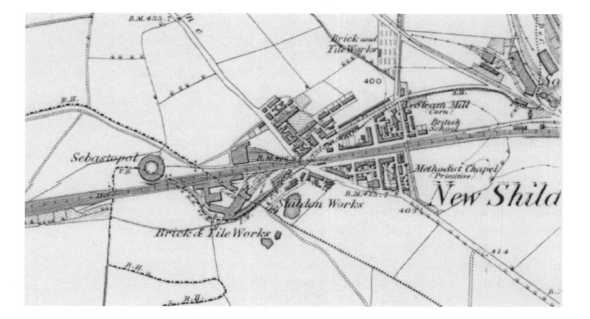

was little development of the original works site, as the focus of the railway had now shifted to Soho Works following the franchise of railway support infrastructure to Timothy Hackworth, but after William Bouch's appointment as Chief Engineer in 1840, attention turned once again to New Shildon Works and it was there that the first identifiably modern engine shed was built.

New Shildon Works had been the home of the company's locomotive fleet right from the beginning. Now the engines were to be provided with decent accommodation. A 9-track fully roofed shed was built in 1849, with the roundhouse known as 'Sebastopol', just to the west, added five years later. 'Sebastopol' was followed by two additional roundhouses at the same location; the first built between 1852 and 1855. The third roundhouse had to wait until the 1886 shed reconstruction. All three were enclosed within the walls of an NER style brick longhouse structure, which survives today.

The last of the three turntables is significant in that it was adapted in 1915 for use by the NER's fleet of ten electric locomotives (see Chapter 10).

The expanding parish of New Shildon (as it appears on the O.S. map of 1898).

It seems from surviving works reports, that the 1849 shed was just a combination and extension of two existing buildings at the same location, most likely the 1838 and 1842 buildings, a practice of 'make do and mend' that continued throughout the company's presence in the town.[10] The location of the roundhouses, east of the Brusselton incline, would, in one guise or another, be the home of Shildon's locomotive fleet for more than a hundred years. The only addition was a temporary 2-track 'through' shed, imported from another S&DR site, and rebuilt near Shildon station in 1852. By 1923, there were 73 locomotives 'stabled' at New Shildon including ten electric locos, of which more later.

When the industrial malaise of the 1930s reduced the nation's need for rail freight, the London and North Eastern Railway (LNER), which now occupied the site, decided to downgrade the extensive marshalling yard east of Shildon station, which at one time was the biggest in the UK. Unfortunately, one additional casualty was the Shildon engine shed.

Shildon, for more than a century, had been the start-point for coal trains from the South Durham coalfield but as coal demand dwindled, the scale of the operation became unsustainable. Without coal trains, there was little need for locomotives and it was decided to close Shildon shed and transfer most of the engines to nearby West Auckland. The engines which were transferred consisted of ten 0-6-0 J21s, one 0-6-0 J23, eleven 0-6-0 J25s, one 0-6-0 J26, three 0-6-0 J27s, five 0-6-0T J71s, one 0-6-0T J72, one N12 0-6-2T, one 0-8-0 Q5, two G5 0-4-4Ts plus the ten freight electrics, which moved to Darlington. The shed finally closed on 8 July 1935 when the buildings were absorbed into the expanding wagon works.[11]

The longhouse, which had housed the three turntables, was converted to a wagon repair shop but would have a belated swansong. During the 150th anniversary celebration of the S&DR in 1975, it became the engine shed it was originally designed to be. For a few short weeks, it was the temporary home of an impressive collection of steam locomotives, making ready to reproduce the S&DR centenary cavalcade of 1925. Nevertheless as soon as the celebrations were over, it reverted to the wagon repair shop it had recently been. It was believed at that time, on the strength of Shildon's impressive manufacturing output, that the Works was destined for a long life. Unfortunately, this was not to be. The historic railway connection to the site was finally severed in 1984 when the works closed for good. Amazingly, the old steam locomotive shed was one of the few buildings from

Shildon railwaymen on shed c.1900, (picture courtesy of Beamish Museum).

the Works to survive on what is now the Hackworth Industrial Estate. The eastern end of the building is currently occupied by Blue Diamond Machine Tools Ltd, and I was fortunate enough to discover that the owner, Brian Burn, was interested in the building's railway history. On a September morning in 2016, in the company of Timothy Hackworth's great-great granddaughter, Jane Hackworth-Young, I was given a guided tour of the old Shildon engine shed. Much of the structure of the original building has survived. Its external appearance is immediately recognisable as a typical NER brick locomotive longhouse. When it was an engine shed the locomotives would have entered by a central road and then parked up in a bay in one of the three roundhouses. The more linear rail system used in 1975 derived from the conversion to a wagon works repair shop in the 1930s. The rails, which once ran beside the shed and terminated at the bottom of the Brusselton incline, are now lifted and have been replaced by a service road for the industrial estate. The land immediately west has been redeveloped and is now a mineral processing works. The shed has retained most of the external features it acquired during its 1886-92 reconstruction. The eastern end of the building has been converted to an engineering machinery showroom although, even so, some of the original features are still recognisable. The familiar series of arched windows, installed in 1886 and running the length of the building, are obvious, even if bricks have since replaced the soot covered glass which was once there. The floor has been re-laid so there is no evidence of the subsurface work pits which replaced the turntables when the building was converted to a wagon works. The rails that ran the length of the building also no longer exist, although their former existence may be inferred from remnants poking through the concrete in the adjacent car park. A wall separates the engineering showroom from the northern half of the longhouse. Notably absent are vents in the roof for locomotive chimney exhaust. They disappeared when the building was re-roofed. There is no visible evidence that the building had once been a series of three roundhouses. Pictures taken just before the Second World War, by which time it had become a wagon repair shop, show parallel sets of rails, so the conversion must have taken place shortly after the building ceased to be a locomotive shed.

The former Shildon engine shed as it is today.

Just inside the doors of the northern half of the building is one intriguing feature. It had once been the toilet and restroom for

the wagon works and, prior to that time, the foreman's office for the engine shed. It is an odd, low-roofed structure, made from stone blocks with anomalous chunks of metal girder protruding from its roof. It has nothing in common with the building in which it is housed and likely predates the rest of the building. The intriguing possibility is that it is a survivor of 'Sebastopol'. If so, it may be one of three similar small buildings on the (then) outside wall of the original roundhouse, as shown on the engine shed plan of 1856. Hopefully, further research will shed light on this. Irrespective of the internal changes which have taken place over the years to the old engine shed, it is pleasing to note that one small but important piece of New Shildon's railway heritage has somehow survived.

S&DR locomotives were housed on or near this location from the beginning. The first was Stephenson's *Locomotion*, or *Locomotive No.1* as it is more commonly referred to in company records. Further engines from Forth Street soon followed, such that by the spring of 1827 there were six working engines seen by the two visiting Prussian engineers. These were the Stephenson 0-4-0s: *Locomotion No 1, Hope, Black Diamond, Diligence* and *Stockton*, with the sixth possibly the experimental engine *Chittaprat*. This erratic performer had been provided on a sale-or-return trial basis by Robert Wilson and Co. of Newcastle. *Chittaprat* was a strange affair; each wheel driven independently from separate cylinders, making the locomotive the first four-cylinder engine in the world. Yet, despite the potential power this might have generated, *Chittaprat* failed to fulfil its promise and was difficult to maintain, being regularly out of service in the two years in which it retained its original structure. The S&DR eventually bought the engine at a knockdown price, so that they could recycle the boiler, whereupon the engine was handed to Timothy Hackworth to use for his own experimental purposes. Stephenson's S&DR engines were unreliable. Their construction was little better than the engines George had sold to Hetton Colliery four years earlier. In consequence, the S&DR management was at a crossroads. From a financial perspective, steam locomotives offered little benefit over horses when purchase and running costs were taken into consideration. So, with the future of steam hanging in the balance, Hackworth decided to completely rebuild *Chittaprat* adapting it to his own design. His aim was to incorporate all the best features of the engines he had worked on over the years, while at the same time incorporate novel ideas of his own.

One of these was the provision of efficient springs, which he both invented and patented. When it emerged from the New Shildon proto-works, the rebuilt *Chittaprat* bore little resemblance to its previous incarnation. Hackworth had converted it from a four-cylinder four-wheeler to a two-cylinder six-wheeler with the wheels coupled together to provide coordinated traction and power. Hackworth also redesigned the boiler, incorporating the efficient 'U' shape flue he had found so beneficial at Wylam. This reduced heat wastage by doubling the heating area available to boil water. Most significantly, Hackworth introduced the first modern blast-pipe, which greatly improved draught through the grate, thus generating extra heat from the fire and banishing the principal fault of Stephenson's engines, which was catastrophic loss of steam pressure whenever the engine was under severe load. There have been many contenders as to who actually invented the 'blast pipe', including Richard Trevithick, William Hedley and George Stephenson, but Hackworth was the first

Hackworth's *Royal George* (picture courtesy of Jane Hackworth-Young).

to define and deliberately exploit the fundamental principles on which the device depended.

The end-product of Hackworth's efforts was arguably the most powerful and reliable freight locomotive seen in the world to date, the *Royal George*. Construction and assembly work was carried out by two S&DR employees, Thomas Dobson (Foreman Smith) and Thomas Taylor (Foreman Fitter), in the open air outside the blacksmith's shop east of the Brusselton incline.[12] It is not stretching imagination too far to say that *Royal George* was the saviour of the steam locomotive since it demonstrated beyond doubt the advantage of steam over horse traction. With the success of *Royal George*, Hackworth was given the freedom to build more locos for the S&DR, of which the first was a *Royal George* clone called *Victory*, which emerged from the same works in 1829.

Also that year, Timothy Hackworth made his own bid for fame. He submitted a locomotive, constructed to his design, to the Rainhill Trials. For those who don't know the background, the proprietors of the railway, then under construction between Liverpool and Manchester, were unconvinced about the long-term benefits of steam traction. There was, for instance, talk of rope-hauled trains, powered by winding engines, as well as the inevitable suggestion of horses. The development of early steam locos had been advanced by the accelerating costs in terms of men and horses caused by the Napoleonic war. When this ended horses and manpower suddenly became cheap and there was less need for an alternative source of motive power.

The proprietors of the L&MR therefore arranged a competition in October 1829, open to all comers, with the object of finding a steam locomotive capable of meeting their pre-determined criteria, which included the provision that the engine should 'effectively consume its own smoke …. and must be capable of drawing a train of carriages weighing 20 tons, day after day, at a speed of 10mph.'

The winner would get £500 and his design would provide the template for steam locomotives on the railway, should that be confirmed as the way forward. Hackworth's most recent experience of building a loco from scratch dated from a brief stint at Stephenson's Forth Street works and the facilities now available bore little resemblance to those at Newcastle. With his New Shildon workshops barely able to handle routine locomotive maintenance, Hackworth had to enlist other engineering companies to make the principal components of his locomotive, which would be called *Sanspareil* (or 'without equal', the name Sanspareil being subject to alternative spellings, it also often appears as 'Sans Pareil' which is the literal French form). The boiler was therefore made at Bedlington Ironworks and, more controversially as it transpired, the cylinders were manufactured at Forth Street. 'Controversially', because Stephenson was also Hackworth's main opposition at Rainhill. Hackworth had based his design on the successful formula employed for *Royal George*, incorporating the tried and tested Wylam 'U' shaped boiler which had proved so effective at both New Shildon and Wylam. Construction, however, proved to be a nightmare of logistics. Fitting in extra-curricular work on *Sanspareil* between other duties, Hackworth left himself with no time to test the machine properly and, more importantly, iron out the faults before the trials began. *Sanspareil* was assembled outside the New Shildon blacksmith's shop and given a cursory work-out during the hours of darkness, a few days before Rainhill. On its first day at Liverpool, it performed as well as the main competitor, Stephenson's *Rocket*, but – and here's where the controversy starts – one of the Stephenson cylinders blew up on the second day enabling *Rocket* to take the prize. The conspiracy argument continues to this day. Yet, despite Hackworth's cries of foul play, *Rocket* was really the superior engine and many of its innovative features, such as the boiler's copper fire tubes, became standard on later steam locomotives – including, it must be noted, those built by Timothy Hackworth. Despite *Sanspareil*'s failure at Rainhill, the owners of the Liverpool and Manchester Railway (L&MR) were sufficiently impressed with its performance to agree to its purchase. It went on to serve the L&MR and the Bolton and Leigh Railway for many years before eventually being converted for use as a snow plough. Apart from its late-night try-out, however, it never worked again at New Shildon. It is therefore ironic that Shildon would become its final resting place. It was restored by John Hick of 'Hick and Hargreaves' and presented to the Patent Office and from there moved to the Science Museum and after years on display at South Kensington, and then the National Railway Museum at York, it ended up close to the site of its construction. It is now displayed at Locomotion, where there is also a replica nearby, which gives a better impression of how it looked on the day it battled with *Rocket* at Rainhill.

In the four years after *Royal George*, six additional engines were supplied to the S&DR, although in most cases the manufacturer and designer was Robert Stephenson. These were '*Experiment*', '*Rocket*', '*Victory*', '*Globe*', '*Planet*' and '*North Star*'. All were meant for heavy freight use apart from *Globe*, which was a light, fast 0-4-0, designed by Hackworth specifically for passenger traffic, as the Company had recently brought passenger conveyance in-house following the railway's extension to Middlesbrough. The only engine to be completely built at New Shildon during this period was *Victory*, reflecting the limitations of space, manpower and equipment at the site. This and the *Sanspareil* experience at Rainhill must have been a source of irritation to Hackworth. Dependent on others to produce engines, over whose construction and design he had little control, he was then expected to maintain them in all good order. As the years went by he became increasingly frustrated. The only sure way, as he saw it, of guaranteeing the quality he needed was to oversee locomotive design and production himself. For that, however, he needed both the capital and the freedom to work independently. Fortunately, by the end of the decade, both were available. So, with his employer's backing, Hackworth began building a loco fleet of his own. Fortuitously, Thomas Greener had returned to the S&DR after a long sabbatical on the Liverpool and Manchester Railway and was able to assist. Like Hackworth, Greener had a longstanding connection to the S&DR. He had initially moved to New Shildon from Newcastle to oversee the construction of the cuttings and embankments for the Etherley incline on behalf of his former work colleague, George Stephenson. The Company was so impressed by his ability they took him on as an engineer, and according to Greener was there in time, 'to see the first rail laid at Stockton'. Having worked on the construction of the incline at Etherley, he was appointed the first operator of the stationary engine there, a job he eventually handed on to his younger brother, John, either late in 1826 or early 1827. He returned to the S&DR at the end of the decade to oversee the new coal staithes at Middlesbrough, allowing Hackworth to concentrate on the Shildon end of the business, which now included locomotive construction.

New workshops appeared in May 1831 and the first Hackworth engines to emerge were, in the tradition of *Royal George*, heavy duty freight 0-6-0s intended for slow-and-steady freight haulage. Locomotive manufacture at New Shildon was nevertheless still in its infancy; the *British Locomotive Catalogue 1825-1923* suggests that all the component parts of the engines were made elsewhere, with only assembly taking place at New Shildon.

Unlike *Royal George*, however, some of the new engines were fitted with copper steam tubes, in the manner of Stephenson's engines. These were classified after the first to emerge, *Majestic*, and proved reliable and efficient workhorses, in contrast to Stephenson's 'Planet' class 2-2-0s, which were underpowered for the heavy work they were expected to do. The Hackworth designed engines were *Majestic, Coronation, William the Fourth, Northumbrian, Lord Brougham* and, the first to carry the name, *Shildon*. Nevertheless, for several more years he continued with his tried and tested 'U' tube boilers on his own freight engines.

Meanwhile, the S&DR were becoming disillusioned with private operators using horses on their rails, which held up and generally frustrated the company's steam trains. The S&DR had been restricted by their charter but reluctantly came to the decision that the only way out of the mess was to buy out the independents. This was going to be costly since the railway was in public ownership and they couldn't just bar existing operators from their tracks without providing compensation. The independent coach operators in 1832 were Pickersgill and Co, Scott and Co, Ludley and Buckton, operating between Stockton and Darlington, Adamson operating between Shildon and Darlington and Wastell operating between Yarm and Stockton. The normal loading for each coach, if you can believe it, was 6 inside and 20 outside.

Despite having made provision for passenger traffic in the 1823 Act of Parliament, the Company had assumed that passenger use would be peripheral to the business of shifting coal and it took them more than 7 years to realise their mistake. Apart from the increase in revenue they could command, they could also co-ordinate train movement better if passenger transport was brought in-house. The independent passenger coaches had certainly acquired notoriety. A Stockton race meeting horse-drawn coach special is reported to have carried forty-six passengers, with just nine paying to travel inside.[13] One of those sights you wish you had seen. Horse-drawn passenger coaches ceased to work the main lines from 1833 when the S&DR introduced its own scheduled steam-hauled service. Horse-drawn coaches continued to operate until, at least, 1840 on sections of the railway where locomotive use was either impractical or not cost-effective, one such example being the section of the railway west of the Brusselton incline. Incidentally, John Glass was the first guard employed on an S&DR passenger train. He wore a red coat for identification.

Following howls of protest from the other coach operators, the company agreed, for a fee, to attach the independents' coaches to the end of their own trains, which must have been worth seeing since some were little more than stagecoaches, with more passengers clinging to the roof than inside. its retinue of passengers clinging on to the roof. It was at this time that the Hackworth-designed *Globe* came into its own. As the flag-ship for the passenger service, it is said to have regularly achieved speeds of up to 50mph in its nine years of operation. *Globe*'s life would end spectacularly with a bang when its boiler exploded in Middlesbrough. With the takeover of passenger services the Company now needed to provide accommodation for their new customers. Part of a warehouse in Shildon was modified to provide a waiting room and attached cottage, which was let out to office staff.[14]

The other improvement, after 1830, was the doubling of single lines and the replacement of the cheap brittle cast-iron rails with those made from malleable iron. It is a measure of how little speed was considered an important factor on the railway that drivers were still being instructed to drive at 'moderate speeds' and stop their train if they saw horses on roads or in fields looking distressed due to the noise created by the engine's exhaust.[15] Always at the back of Hackworth's mind was Stephenson's influence over the Railway and the latter's dubious legacy in terms of the unreliable engines he had supplied. The locomotive manufacturing process sorely needed to be kept in-house; even those engines currently assembled by Hackworth at New Shildon were dependent upon parts manufactured elsewhere. This situation was about to change.

CHAPTER FIVE

Timothy Hackworth and Soho Works

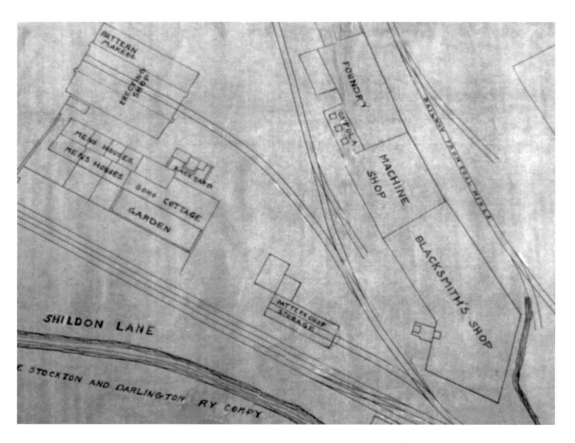

Layout of Soho Works (reproduced from the 1853 sale documents).

Using money from the sale of his mother's house in Wylam and a £9,000 loan from the Pease family, Hackworth took the courageous decision to set up his own engineering and locomotive works.[16] The site he settled upon was a mile east of the S&DR works, immediately north of where Shildon railway station is today. The location was strategically chosen. The land where the works would be built was at the junction of three railways; the S&DR line from Brusselton, the Black Boy branch line to Black Boy Colliery, and the short, privately owned, Surtees line from the Surtees family's colliery at Shildon Lodge. Hackworth approached the proprietors of the S&DR with a proposition; that he would cease acting as their 'superintendent' but, instead, become an independent contractor, but one totally responsible for ensuring traffic movement, locomotive manufacture and maintenance, with everything that entailed, including the management of the stationary engine driven inclines. During his time as contractor he leased Shildon Works from the S&DR, which continued operating under his management. However, fundamental to the new arrangement was the creation of his own Soho Works. There are several claims as to the origin of the name 'Soho Works', but perhaps the most likely is that it was borrowed from that already used by the well-known and well-respected establishment operated by Boulton and Watt in Birmingham.

S&DR locomotives, whenever possible, would no longer be bought from other manufacturers or assembled from parts produced elsewhere. From now on they would be built at New Shildon in their entirety, so that every aspect of their production could be overseen. To this end, new workshops and a foundry arose along

Soho Works' blacksmith's shop, foundry and machine shops (1947 LNER picture).

with a locomotive manufacturing shop at Soho Works. Other engineering, including such matters as wagon building and rolling stock maintenance, were divided between the old site and the new, works, with the old works remaining in the ownership of the S&DR albeit managed by Hackworth. The wet land on the opposite side of the rails from Soho Works was already under development. A storehouse for metal had been raised by Kilburn's Iron Works, and was used for storing iron destined for the future S&DR wagon works.[17] Although owned (at least in part) by Timothy Hackworth, the management of Soho Works was handed to his younger brother, Thomas. Thomas, like his sibling, had served his apprenticeship at Wylam Colliery in Northumberland and was involved, in some capacity, in the construction of all the legendary Wylam 'travelling engines', including *Puffing Billy* and *Wylam Dilly*. He even followed in Timothy's footsteps to Walbottle Colliery, where he took over from him as Foreman Blacksmith, after Timothy left to join the S&DR. Thomas, now aged 28, was therefore well qualified to deputise for his brother on the engineering side of railway business. His problem, if there was one, was his limited experience with finance. This he partly rectified by taking on Nicholas Downing as a partner. Downing already owned the Phoenix iron foundry at the top of the nearby Black Boy Incline and may have contributed financially towards the creation of Soho Works. He certainly brought with him much useful metal foundry and financial expertise. The enterprise overseen by the two men was duly named Hackworth and Downing. From then on the boundary between what was known as 'Soho Works' and what was 'Hackworth and Downing' (H&D) is somewhat blurred. While Thomas Hackworth claimed he managed both enterprises, Timothy's son John later disputed this, and it may be there was some independence between these two arms of Timothy's empire. The best guess is that the foundry, always referred to as 'Soho Foundry', was managed separately. Judging from S&DR accountant's records of the time, Hackworth and Downing and Soho Works (or sometimes Soho Foundry) were regularly billed as separate and distinct operations. Nevertheless Thomas Hackworth always claimed he was responsible for both. How the incoming work was allocated between Hackworth and Downing, New Shildon Works, and Soho Works, if indeed the latter was a separate operation, is not clear although it is known from extant locomotive manufacturing details that all these various parts of Hackworth's domain contributed. Since Timothy Hackworth had overall control of all the plants, one assumes that he divided up the projects according to the best use of workshop space, manpower, and plant available at any time. What is certain is that between 1835 and 1840, 14 new locomotives were produced at Shildon; all nominally attributable to Hackworth and Downing, regardless of where their component parts had been synthesised. Roughly half of the output from Hackworth and Downing, however, was not intended for the S&DR. This included three locomotives that went to Canada and another which was shipped to Russia. The Russian engine pay bills, suggest that the only part of the locomotive directly attributable to 'Hackworth and Downing' was the tender with the rest assigned vaguely to 'Soho Works'. These unusual and ground-breaking exports had their own fascinating stories to tell.

The three Canadian engines were purchased by the Albion Mining Company of Nova Scotia, on the behest of the London based engineering firm of George and John Rennie. By the third decade of the nineteenth century, the Rennie brothers were famous throughout the land as railway engineers. John, later Sir John, Rennie had acted as surveyor for the original Darlington to Stockton canal proposal, years before the railway scheme was proposed. He knew the S&DR's father figure George Stephenson well, having worked, albeit reluctantly, alongside him on the construction of the Liverpool and Manchester Railway. It is clear from Rennie's memoirs that he and Stephenson didn't get on. Sir John had no time for self-educated engineers with strong regional accents, particularly those chosen in preference to himself on major railway projects.

Thomas Hackworth.

Who recommended 'Hackworth and Downing' to Rennie isn't recorded, but his request to the North-East company for help probably resulted from his own works being overcommitted and therefore unable to accommodate a time-consuming and potentially loss-making Canadian adventure.

It therefore fell to the men of New Shildon to manufacture the locomotives for the first Canadian steam powered freight railway. The Shildon engines weren't the first locomotives to work in that country; that honour belonged to Robert Stephenson, who had built an engine for the first Canadian railway, a line between Montreal and Lake Champlain in New York state. Nevertheless, the Montreal outfit was a modest affair intended solely for passenger traffic, and lost money from the day it opened. The railway in which Soho Works became involved was a more substantial affair. It could usefully be compared with the S&DR, in its early years, being created to move coal from the collieries to the coast, in this case from Albion Mines in Nova Scotia to the Atlantic port of Picton. If there was anywhere in North America that needed coal at the time it was Picton. The port had been constructed to facilitate coal exports to the USA but was also a popular refuelling port for ocean-going vessels, a factor which the railway proprietors hoped to exploit.

John Buddle, a South Hetton mine owner, acted as intermediary between Canada and Britain, and one of the three engines supplied by Hackworth duly bore his name. The others were *Samson* and *Hercules*, and all were typical Hackworth heavy freight 0-6-0s like those which worked out of New Shildon. All were shipped out in April 1839 along with their drivers, also supplied by Soho Works. In addition to the engines, Soho Works provided most of the fixtures and fittings for the railway, including the Canadian company's only locomotive turntable. All the Shildon exports seem to have performed admirably and gave many years of useful service on the other side of the pond. *Samson* even went on to front the royal train used by Queen Victoria's son Alfred during his visit in 1851. It was fitting therefore that, of the three, it was *Samson* which survived. When its days as a working engine ended, it was sent to the USA where it was to be displayed at the Exposition of Chicago at the instigation of the person running it, Timothy Hackworth Young, the grandson of Timothy Hackworth. It was many years before it finally returned home to Nova Scotia, but it is now on display at the Nova Scotia Museum of Industry at Stellarton. Ironically, apart from the experimental *Sanspareil*, *Samson* on the other side of the Atlantic is the only surviving locomotive known for certain to have been both designed and built by Hackworth at New Shildon.

The other notable engine to emerge from Soho Works during the thirties, however, was a typical Stephenson long boiler 'Patentee' 2-2-2 design. It was a passenger locomotive intended for the Tsar of Russia. The story of the Russian engine has been retold many times (not least by myself) but may be summarised as follows; Tsar Nicholas I, impressed by what he saw as a youngster in England, determined to introduce a steam powered railway to Russia. Amongst the companies he approached to supply locomotives for his railway, designed to connect St. Petersburg to his summer palace in Tsarskoye Selo (sometimes spelt 'Tsarkoye Selo' and 'Tsarskoe Selo'), was Robert Stephenson and Co. Stephenson, as with Rennie and the Canadian project, had more work than he could handle but was reluctant to pass on what might be a lucrative future market. He therefore contracted the production of two of the four engines he was asked to provide to Soho Works. Hackworth also recognised the potential such a contract might bring and set to work with a vengeance, such that, despite his late involvement, the first engine ready for delivery came from the Shildon workshops. It was broken down, packed into crates, and shipped out to Russia in October 1836. It turned out to be a perilous journey.

The boat on which the engine was being carried ran into pack ice in the Baltic and was forced to seek shelter at the nearest available ice-free port. Wooden sledges were built on the dockside and the crated engine, with its accompanying entourage of Shildon railwaymen, set out to cross the snowbound countryside. The party had to endure many hardships along the way. Apart from bivouacking each night in sub-zero conditions, they had to fight off attacks from packs of hungry wolves. By the time they arrived at their destination they found that some of the engine parts had succumbed to the extreme cold and needed urgent repairs which meant a further hazardous journey through snow to Moscow, by one of the engineers, to seek out a manufacturer for a replacement cylinder. Throughout all this, the most remarkable aspect of the project was that the expedition was led by Timothy Hackworth's son, John, who was only sixteen at the time.

The engine was put together at Tsarskoye Selo and performed well in trials. However, if the Tsar was impressed by what he saw, he made no attempt to build on what he had until many years later and, crucially, didn't purchase the second Stephenson engine currently under construction at Shildon. Although there is no definitive proof, this almost certainly became the controversial engine *Arrow*, which will be discussed later. If there was to be a legacy from the expedition, it concerned John Wesley Hackworth who was destined to become a great engineer in his own right. From letters he penned later, it is clear he considered the Russian adventure as his personal passage to adulthood and for the rest of his life he sported an unfashionable Russian style beard in memory of his great adventure. In respect of the normal output from Soho Works, however, the locomotives for Russia and Canada were the exception rather than the rule. Its biggest customer was still the S&DR and, since the S&DR was still pulling the strings, there were none built in this period for local rivals such as the Clarence

Inside and outside Soho Works just prior to demolition (pictures courtesy Jane Hackworth-Young).

Railway, although railway companies outside the S&DR immediate field of interest were considered fair game.

Locomotive manufacture was just part of the work undertaken by Hackworth on behalf of the S&DR. All the stationary engines on the standing inclines were maintained by Hackworth and Downing. The big exception was the routine repairs to S&DR rolling stock which remained within the remit of Shildon Works. Towards the end of the 1830s, coal wagon production began there in earnest. Initially introduced as a stop gap, whenever demand exceeded stocks, there was now a pressing need for in-house manufacture to meet customers' expectations. Wagon assembly centred on Shildon Works but Hackworth and Downing, or more specifically the Soho Foundry, provided important components including axles and wheels. Coal production in Central Durham was increasing year on year and demand for new locomotives was such that Soho Works could not provide the majority of the engines the Company needed. By the end of the decade, manufacture of most of the S&DR fleet had been outsourced. Nevertheless, it is a testament to the perceived reliability and efficiency of Hackworth's engines that these engines were still being made according to Hackworth's design and specification. Maintenance of all the locomotives remained at New Shildon and the original S&DR site expanded accordingly. In consequence, workshops across the town were buzzing. It must therefore have come as a shock to Hackworth's brother Thomas, when in March 1837, his partner and financial support jumped ship. What brought about the termination of the partnership isn't recorded but it seems likely that Nicholas Downing had just spread his personal empire a little too thin. His Phoenix foundry, just up the road in Old Shildon, had more work than it could cope with and Downing was in the process of launching a similar venture in Stockton-on-Tees. Whatever his reason for quitting, however, his departure couldn't have come at a worse time. Thomas Hackworth, a more than competent engineer, had little aptitude for finance and his business, now titled 'Thomas Hackworth and Co,' began a slow slide downhill. This seems to have been an unfortunate family characteristic. His more famous brother made little from any of the enterprises he invested in or oversaw. The first blow to Soho Works was the calling in of the remaining £1700 of the loan provided by the Quakers in order to create Soho Works.

It is clear from S&DR committee notes that Thomas was never flavour of the month at the S&DR. He was accused at various times throughout his five years tenure of providing a poor service, particularly in respect of the maintenance of rolling stock and stationary engines. The management of Brusselton incline came within Thomas's remit and an unfortunate sequence of accidents between 1837 and 1839 was attributed to negligence by Thomas's people. The final straw was when the S&DR refused to accept the engine built at Soho Works known as the *Arrow*. It had started life, almost certainly, as the second engine intended for the Russian Tsar, but after the Tsar lost interest it was sold to the S&DR as a passenger engine. It performed poorly during trials. Robert Young, in his biography of Timothy Hackworth, says of *Arrow* that it 'did very good service' achieving speeds of up to 60mph. It may well have done, but certainly not during the trial period when Thomas, with mounting debts, was desperate for a sale. Complaints, followed by costly modifications, dragged on for a year, with the S&DR refusing to accept the engine until all the faults had been addressed. Existing on a typical Hackworth marginal budget, this did little for the perilous bank balance of Thomas Hackworth and Co and debts began to mount. As a short-term measure, the Pease family reluctantly agreed to accept interest-only repayments on their loan until the financial side of Thomas's company could be sorted out, probably because they wished to retain the services of Timothy Hackworth. This concession, however, came with its own conditions. The down-side was that the S&DR were now back in the driving seat and able to dictate their own terms on how Thomas's company should operate. This included a restriction on work undertaken on behalf of the S&DR's competitors such as the Clarence Railway whose requests for loco repairs was vetoed by the S&DR. Since Thomas had been able to charge the going rate for extracurricular work, this was a massive financial blow. At the end of 1839, and apparently with little warning, Thomas was summarily ousted from his position as manager of Soho Works and simultaneously evicted from his home, Soho Cottage, which he shared with his brother. It is perhaps possible he had an inkling of what was about to happen before the axe fell as he asked the S&DR, a few weeks before his departure, about the possibility of buying land from them opposite Shildon Works, ostensibly for a new factory.[18] His brother had seen the writing on the wall much earlier in the year. In April, he had approached the S&DR with the object of ending his contract with them and taking over direct control of Soho Works. Initially racked with doubt about the viability of his company, his

Hackworth's 0-6-0 *Leader*, built at Soho Works in 1842.

first reaction after taking over from his brother was to cut his losses and put the Works up for sale. An advertisement duly appeared in the October edition of the *Newcastle Courant* which luckily for us provides a neat account of exactly what Soho Works amounted to at that time. Amongst the constituent parts up for grabs were, a 'freehold iron foundry, pattern and smith's shops and a shade for erecting locomotive engines'. That locomotives were still being assembled under a 'shade', exposed to the elements, suggests that locomotive manufacture was still seen by Timothy as an adjunct to the core business, which was day-to-day provision and maintenance of S&DR rolling stock and heavy engineering equipment.

Thomas, meanwhile, quickly abandoned the idea of setting up his own business at Shildon and moved away to Stockton where, in partnership with a man called George Fossick, who would later have a chequered career in the partnership, established his own engineering business. Apart from locomotives, and he may have produced as many as a hundred engines in the quarter of a century he was there, his company, Fossick and Hackworth, also made rolling stock parts such as wheels and axles for wagons, including those being built at Shildon. Ironically, given his acrimonious departure from New Shildon, many of these components were supplied to the S&DR. Additionally the first locomotive to emerge from the Stockton works appropriately named Stockton was bought by the S&DR, although this may have been the completion of some Soho Works contractual debt repayment agreement.

His particular innovation, however, was to oversee the company's transition to steam-ship engine production. Later called Blair and Co. the company prospered and became the main employer in Stockton over the following century.

Statue of Timothy Hackworth at 'Locomotion', Shildon, in front of his *Sanspareil*.

Back at Soho Works, Timothy Hackworth had had a change of heart and decided to try and resurrect the fortunes of his company. While he hadn't foresworn doing work for the S&DR, having severed his contractual ties, he now felt able to venture further afield and take on more lucrative offers of work. Although Hackworth officially left the S&DR in May 1840 but was still occupying buildings belonging to the S&DR a year later, suggesting that his standing with the S&DR was higher than his brother's.

CHAPTER SIX

Bouch, Gilkes and the final months of the S&DR

In November 1839, Timothy Hackworth was formally requested to quit Shildon Shops. In the ensuing six months the owners appointed his replacement.[19] The Board of Directors report of the S&DR for 8 May 1840 stated:

> 'Oswald Gilkes attended this Committee and stated that he, and William Bouch, entered upon the company's shops on the 1st of this month under the name of the "Shildon Works Company".'

Gilkes (the manager) and Bouch (the foreman) were now in charge of Shildon Works, operating under similar terms of reference as Hackworth had in the 1820s, albeit without the support of Soho Works, which continued to operate with Timothy at the helm as before. The Gilkes family, also Quakers like the Pease family, originated from Nailsworth in Gloucestershire, and were well known in Shildon. Nicholas Downing was about to sell Phoenix Foundry to Edgar Gilkes, and Edgar, after a spell under his older brother's tutelage, would soon set up his own S&DR railway works, Gilkes, Wilson and Co, at Middlesbrough at the tender age of 22. Within ten years, this company employed more than 200 men, manufacturing several locomotives for the S&DR, including the fraternally titled engine *Oswald Gilkes*. Perhaps, more controversially, his company supplied much of the substandard metal work used on the infamous Tay Bridge. Oswald Gilkes' partner William Bouch was the younger brother of Thomas Bouch, who would earn even more notoriety than Edgar Gilkes, being the actual designer of the bridge, which collapsed in a storm at the end of 1879, killing all 75 passengers aboard the night mail.

During the time Timothy Hackworth was responsible for the upkeep of the company's stationary and travelling engines, the S&DR work

William Bouch.

Soho Cottage, late nineteenth century. The railway lines in front of the house belonged to the Surtees branch which no longer exists (picture courtesy Jane Hackworth-Young).

had been divided between Soho Works and the S&DR workshops to the west; the division based loosely on availability of manpower and plant. However, not long after his departure Shildon Works Company began building locomotives on the S&DR's original site, and to their own specification. The engines were nominally Bouch designs but were, at least in the beginning, Stephenson/Hackworth hybrids, having the robust appearance, 0-6-0 wheel-arrangement and familiar sloping cylinders of the Hackworth fleet, but augmented by a long boiler in the style of the latest engines emerging from Robert Stephenson's Newcastle factory. Of the fifteen locos built by the Company (SWC) between 1840 and 1850, six are notable, in the context of this book, as being remembered as the 'Shildon Class'. These were S&DR numbers 29 *Miner*, 30 *Wear*, 31 *Redcar*, 32 *Eldon*, 33 *Shildon* and 34 *Driver*, with three similar engines built two years later, numbers 35 *Commerce*, 36 *Guisborough* and 37 *Gem*.

Three of Bouch's engines were later exhibited at Darlington during the S&DR golden jubilee celebration in 1875. They were number 50 *Meteor*, 35 *Commerce* and, appropriately enough 38 *Shildon*; the nearest Shildon got to taking an active part in the festivities.[20]

One of the first things Bouch and Gilkes did on taking charge was to build the Company's first recognisable engine shed. This is referenced in the Works report of 28 April 1841 as follows:

'an engine shed 120 feet by 42 feet, capable of holding 16 engines with their water barrels can be erected and made complete, with the exception of the engineers' work, for the sum of £300.'

The 1841 building, referred to in minutes as the 'spare shed', seems to have been a template for the building built by the NER in 1890, still there today, in that it had a three-gabled roof structure.[21] Unfortunately, the exact location is not recorded, nor is there any indication of where it was from surviving records. The likelihood is that it was located on the same site as the 9-track shed, which appeared eight years later, since this was conveniently situated alongside the SWC works. The *British Shed Directory* also records a 2-track through engine shed, built in 1852, on the opposite side of the railway line to the longhouse structure still there today. Given the way the wagon works developed, this building may also have been adapted and incorporated into the expanding workshops in the same way as the longhouse.

These were not the only immediate changes made by the incoming management team. The oddest entry in committee reports, perhaps, details alterations to the 'recently vacated house belonging to Timothy Hackworth'. The changes amounted to conversion of Hackworth's 'recently vacated' house into three 'tenements' for workmen. *The Northern Echo* of 19 November 1897 also reported the recently 'razed' two storey house formerly occupied by Timothy Hackworth.

Which house this was is a mystery since Hackworth is understood to have lived in Soho Cottage from the moment it was built until the day he died in July 1850. Soho Cottage is still there today and was sold by Hackworth's surviving children, along with Soho Works. It seems reasonable to assume therefore, it was in Timothy's ownership at the time he died. Whether or not it belonged to him, wholly or partly, ten years earlier is a different matter. There is the possibility he only completed the purchase of Soho Cottage from the S&DR, who built it, after severing formal ties with his ex-employer. The best guess regarding the 'recently vacated' 1840 Hackworth house, mentioned in Company records, was it was the two storey property near Brusselton incline which Hackworth occupied before Soho Cottage was built, and was subsequently demolished in 1897.

Platelayers' and bank riders' cabins showing gasometer to left (1947 LNER picture).

In the summer of 1845, moves were made by the S&DR to establish a gas works in the town. Initially this was meant to be located near New Shildon tunnel where continuous lighting was needed by the Company, but the coal gas plant was eventually built on a more convenient site next to Soho Works, 'between John Graham's house and the Black Boy Incline'.[22] The aim was to produce coal gas primarily for the S&DR, who financed the factory's construction and the motive force behind the scheme was an experienced gas engineer, George Emett. The Works were completed the following year, with the SWC identified as the nominal owners, and given 'liberty to sell gas on such terms as they and the Committee deem fair and reasonable'.[23] Outside the Railway there were few takers initially, yet within a decade, demand on the Works was such that larger premises were needed, and the operation expanded into the western end of the former Soho Works buildings, Soho long having ceased to be of interest to new owners, the NER. The Railway's Gas Works would eventually become the main provider of coal gas in the town. It supplied the power which lit both streets and homes, cooking the meals and warming the houses of local people well into the twentieth century.

The S&DR was also the town's first supplier of clean water. Before the Industrial Revolution, the main water source for people in the old town had been the nearest available beck (stream), three of which rolled down the 'shield' onto the land which became New Shildon. With the arrival of industry, private wells were sunk from which water could be bought, although at a price few local people could afford. The becks, therefore, continued to be the main fresh water source, becoming overused for both drinking and sewage disposal purposes. This had the inevitable consequence of cholera and other water-borne diseases, which were regular visitors to the town throughout the Victorian age. Since the railway was essentially powered by steam, a source of clean water was a priority for the S&DR right from the start. At one time Shildon based locomotives alone used 150,000 gallons of water a day. Reservoirs had to be created by the Company just to serve the stationary engines at the top of Etherley and Brusselton Hills before the Railway began operating. On the boggy land below Brusselton, storage tanks were filled from streams and utilised as much as possible until 1834, when a formal agreement was signed with Hackworth and Downing(H&D), to supply water solely for 'cleaning locomotives and filling engine boilers'. A metered storage tank (known as a cistern) was installed beside the line on a spoil heap next to their Works.[24] Since it was in H&D's interest at the time to reduce the water table beneath its factory, this was doubly beneficial to H&D. With the transition to steam haulage complete and business booming, the S&DR demand for water soon outstripped supply and the Company were forced to look for alternative sources. Fortunately, the construction of the New Shildon tunnel provided the answer.

The Black Boy incline, which sloped steeply down the shield, had handled coal movement from Black Boy Colliery to the north from 1827. Black Boy was part owned by Jonathan Backhouse, one of the S&DR directors, who therefore had a foot in both the Colliery and Railway camps. The branch line to his Colliery joined up with the main line to Darlington near Soho Works. Aside from coal, the Black Boy branch line also catered for horse-drawn passenger coaches from Bishop Auckland. A standing engine and rope worked incline, similar to Brusselton, replaced the horse-drawn coaches and wagons within a year of the opening, water for the engine at the top of the hill being supplied from a metred cistern. The stationary engine proved a costly investment. The worked incline had been in use for barely a decade before the Company decided to bypass it altogether. The new plan was to excavate a 1,225 yard tunnel directly under the shield to link up with the Bishop Auckland and Weardale Railway (BA&W), north and west of Old Shildon. The cost of the tunnel would be borne jointly by both the S&DR and BA&W whose customers regularly complained about the delays caused to their wagons having to join the queue to ride the inclines. The S&DR also stood to benefit from increased trade, which now included additional revenue from passenger traffic. Construction work on the tunnel, under the guidance of Thomas Storey, now an outside consultant engineer, and overseen on the ground by John Harris, began towards the end of 1839, with the work let out in eight distinct blocks to local contractors. Although it is not known how this was to be accomplished, existing practice was to sink shafts at intervals along the line of the tunnel and then work from the base outwards to meet teams working towards them from adjacent shafts.

George Harker and the proprietors of Adelaide Colliery, west of Shildon, agreed to provide the lining bricks, but the contractor's thirst for bricks soon outstripped the quantity Harker and Adelaide were able to supply. The S&DR, therefore, made new arrangements. They would raise their own brickworks close to the tunnel. This is shown on the 1855 O.S. map to the north and west of the tunnel entrance. All the constituents of bricks other than clay, however, would have to be imported, as none were available in sufficient quality or quantity nearby.

These were not the only problems to be overcome.

The idea of a brickworks owned and managed by the S&DR, unsurprisingly, upset the nominated suppliers who demanded compensation, citing loss of revenue. As if this wasn't enough Adelaide Colliery also sued for damages, arguing they were now unable to work the 'pillars of coal' under their land because of instability problems caused by the tunnel excavation work.[25] Water ingress, too, became a problem. The excavation proceeded in fits and starts, regularly delayed by water rushing in through the porous limestone roof. In consequence, heavy-duty pumps were brought in, and these worked continuously round the clock to allow the work to continue. Unfortunately, this partial solution to the water problem had an unexpected side-effect. Within weeks of the commencement of pumping, a nearby well, which had produced the only clean drinking water for Old Shildon, ran dry. This was situated in Smithson's field, opposite Chapel Row (now Church Street), virtually over the tunnel. The S&DR therefore now had to find the townsfolk an alternative drinking water supply. As a stopgap measure, the Company leased water from an existing, if overworked, industrial well in the nearby Phoenix Foundry. The Phoenix well was already working flat out and had to be enlarged to cope with this unexpected increase in demand. This was probably the well that originally supplied water to the stationary engine at the top of the Black Boy incline, used by the S&DR before the agreement with Hackworth and Downing for water supply in 1834.

The water from the well was pumped to a holding and metering tank, from where it was distributed to the town's residents. In one of those coincidences that seemed to follow the S&DR in their quest for water, this well was owned by Thomas Hackworth's erstwhile partner, Nicholas Downing. Downing must have felt a strange sense of deja vu when requested to provide water to the S&DR, in this instance up to 10,000 gallons/day. The quality of the water provided however left much to be desired. Following numerous complaints from Shildon residents the works committee were instructed to find an alternative source, including pumping water from nearby streams.

It may be recalled that it was H&D who had originally supplied the water that kept Shildon Works humming, but unlike his former partner Thomas Hackworth, Downing maintained a good relationship with the S&DR. In 1846 he even bought both the '*Magnet*' and '*Lord Durham*' engines second-hand from the company, for use in his Foundry. Water management would be a recurring theme for the tunnel project up to and beyond the moment of its completion. Barely four years after the tunnel opened, water roared in through a fissure in the roof and flooded the line. The problem attributed in works reports as due to the 'nearness of Edward Forster's quarry'.

A nearby surface water stream which ran down the hill on the east side of the tunnel, in spate during winter months, was deemed to be the cause, and it was channelled away from the tunnel approach. South of the tunnel, the stream was fed into a concrete aqueduct and directed towards the Works, where it could possibly be used. The contract for the aqueduct construction was handed to the ubiquitous George Harker, who seems to have made a good living out of S&DR work. In addition to the aqueduct, Harker also built a road bridge over the same cutting and, while undertaking tunnel accommodation work, also found time to refurbish the Soho Cottages, which were to be leased to railway workers.[26] The Harker aqueduct is still there, although it now looks an anomalous feature in the landscape, since it seems to be water-free. The stream it was designed to accommodate may indeed always have been a seasonal flow. It was later used to power a corn mill on the north side of Shildon Works. With the redirection of the stream towards the works, the S&DR now had more water than they could handle and even offered to supply water, 'as neighbours', free of charge to Hackworth's Soho Works.[27] The wheel had turned full circle; the S&DR was now the supplier and Hackworth the customer. However, it would be many years before the question of a clean water supply for the town was finally resolved when reservoirs were built by the railway company on land at Waskerley, and Tunstall, near Stanhope, with pipes laid from the reservoir to Shildon. Even this proved to be not as pure as hoped. It transpired that it had been augmented with water from a nearby reservoir owned by the Weardale Iron Company which on occasions allowed sewage to be fed into it.

The first party to officially travel the length of the tunnel, in January 1842, was the Company's railway committee, which included Joseph Pease, representing the family who had built the railway of which the tunnel was now part. It was officially opened on 10 January, with a brass band procession and a baptism of wine on the last brick laid. The candlelit tunnel echoed to the mellow sound of a local marching brass band; an impromptu concert that must have been worth hearing as band members stumbled along the track in the dark.[28] The first passenger train (albeit horse drawn) went through the tunnel in April the same year and steam-hauled freight trains followed the next month. The now redundant stationary engine on the top of the hill (Black Boy engine) was scheduled to be dismantled and its component parts transferred to a new standing incline at Crook.[29] Another branch line from West Auckland was authorised. This connected with the Bishop Auckland line just north of the tunnel and effectively rendered the Brusselton incline redundant, although it continued to be used intermittently as a back-up to the West Auckland line for another 13 years. The steep gradient of the trackbed north of the tunnel proved difficult for freight locomotives, to the extent that there was even talk of providing another stationary engine to assist trains travelling on to Bishop Auckland.[30] Since this would have been a retrograde step, given the reasoning behind the tunnel's existence, the compromise position was the deployment of a banking engine, which was maintained in steam nearby to assist if needed.

Tunnel accidents when they occur throughout history are notorious for loss of life and the Black Boy tunnel was destined to be the scene of a particularly scary near-miss. On Friday, 27 August 1880, the 7.30 eight coach passenger train from Bishop Auckland, for some unexplained reason, jumped the rails north of the tunnel. The derailed coaches, with 50 people on board, stayed upright, but ploughed on into the tunnel for 200 metres before coming to a halt. In the near darkness, panic ensued, inflamed by an erroneous rumour that another train had also entered the tunnel and was about to collide with the wreckage. Passengers able to get out of the coaches jumped down onto the rails and ran back towards the tunnel entrance, blocking access to railway staff coming the other way to assist. The guard, who had been hurled the length of

The Shildon aqueduct.

his van by the collision, tried to bring order to the chaos despite being injured. In the best railway tradition, he took control of the situation and led the passengers through the darkness, smoke and wreckage to safety. For this he received an official commendation. Miraculously the pipework supplying gas lighting to the train remained intact, otherwise there would almost certainly have been a fire with consequences that don't bear thinking about. The train travellers that day were fortunate; somehow, they escaped serious injury. If any of the coaches had hit the walls of the tunnel abutments this could have resulted in one of the major rail accidents of the age. As it was, the only problem in the aftermath of the event was a tunnel blockage. For the following weeks trains from Bishop Auckland were diverted over the Black Boy incline again, as in the old days. Apart from the derailment, the tunnel mostly led an untroubled life, the exception being one day in June 1865 when 0-6-0 no. 120 *Brough* exploded within, seriously injuring the footplate crew.[31]

The 14:50 Shildon to Bishop Auckland train heads north out of Shildon tunnel, 11 February 2018.

With the opening of the tunnel, and the start of uninterrupted passenger conveyance between Darlington and Bishop Auckland, the station at the Mason's Arms crossing, which consisted of one platform and a waiting room on the opposite side of the rail/road junction became redundant. For a time it had doubled as the library and reading room of the Railway Institute. A temporary platform was built just beyond the tunnel cutting. For a time, the Mason's Arms acted as the ticket office for passengers from Shildon, a function a nearby post office would later perform while a purpose-built ticket office was constructed.[32] The Mason's Arms seems to have always played some part in Shildon's railway history. Surprisingly, therefore, it is unclear when the pub was built. It is known to have leased accommodation, including an office and a passenger waiting room, to the S&DR in March 1837 and it looks likely that it was owned by the railway before that because when it went up for sale in 1835 the seller, Ralph Forster, nominated Thomas Storey, the S&DR Engineer/Surveyor, as the first contact for enquiries. Included in the sale was an inn, brewery, stabling, granary, 'byer', yard, four dwelling houses on the north side of the inn, two dwelling houses with yards on the east side of the inn and four plots of land. One of these plots was already being used by the Company as a 'landing place' for merchandise, with a short section of rail linking it to the nearby main line, suggesting the Mason's Arms had more than just incidental connections to the railway company.[33]

The temporary (1842) incarnation of Shildon Station was replaced, in 1860, with the first appearance of a more conventional station on the same site. This was, by all accounts, a ramshackle affair with what passed as a waiting room/ticket office consisting of a corrugated iron shed located on a spoil heap some distance from the platforms. Proposals were made to build another station nearer the end of the tunnel cutting but nothing came of them. In fact, a decent station for the town would have to wait until 1899 when, following repeated complaints from the town council, the iron shed was replaced by decent brick-built waiting rooms, toilets and a ticket office; a typical rural station of the time, not earth shattering by national standards but at least an improvement on the windswept study in reinforced concrete you see today.[34] For 20 years, up until his death in 1884, the station master there was John Glass, the same John Glass whose brother was so tragically killed in the early days of the S&DR. According to the *Middlesbrough Daily Gazette*, Glass had been present when the first rails were laid in 1822 and had travelled in one of the open wagons behind *Locomotion No.1* on the Railway's opening day. Shildon men may have had a reputation for being bolshie but they were nonetheless loyal.[35]

Further improvements to the railway infrastructure were on the cards. Anyone visiting the railway museum at Shildon today, particularly those who take the infrequent short steam rides from the large exhibits building to the former NER goods depot, will be impressed by what remains of the S&DR coal drop. This structure was even bigger in its day. Coal wagons were shunted to the top and their contents discharged down chutes into the tenders of locomotives. Coal drops were once a common feature on railways, nearly always located next to engine sheds. The Shildon example may be one of the largest of these drops to have survived, capable of loading four locomotive tenders at any one time.[36] The Shildon coal drop designed and built by Bouch dates from 1846.

Meanwhile, over at Soho Works, Hackworth was using his new-found freedom to manufacture railway machinery, including

The Bouch-designed coal drops at Locomotion prior to recent restoration and conservation work.

steam engines, for companies wholly unconnected to his former employer. Promotional literature went out to railway companies across the country, including an approach to the Liverpool and Manchester Railway, who had purchased Hackworth's *Sanspareil* following the Rainhill trials, despite its shortcomings on the big day.[37] Although his main customers were local collieries, they also for the first time included the S&DR's principal competitor for the transport of South Durham coal, the hated Clarence Railway. It is a questionable point, in retrospect, whether striking deals with S&DR's main opposition was a good move given Hackworth's financial situation, which was questionable at best. His most obvious customer, given the proximity of his works to the S&DR, was his erstwhile employer, and at the beginning of the Bouch/Gilkes tenure they were inviting tenders for engineering work from all and sundry. Perhaps the CR link was the reason Soho Works was always at the back of the queue whenever S&DR contracts were being handed out. Nevertheless, oblivious to the potential consequences, the first two engines to emerge from Soho Works, *Coxhoe* and *Evenwood*, went to the CR. Over the following decade, of the 35 locomotives built at Soho Works, only three were bought by the Shildon Works Company. Weakening the ties with the S&DR denied Soho Works access to the north-east biggest spender, something Hackworth would have cause to regret. If a decent and fair man, Timothy was not the shrewdest businessman, and, in the light of events, his decision to build engines for the London, Brighton and South Coast Railway (LBSCR) was downright disastrous.

Under the terms of the LBSCR contract, Hackworth was required to supply 14 locomotives, the specification for which would be provided by the Company's engineer, John Gray. They were all 2-2-2 passenger engines and unlike anything manufactured by Hackworth before, unless you count the two Stephenson engines built for the Tsar. The eighteen-month period in which the LBSCR locomotives were being built at Soho Works was possibly the worst time of Hackworth's life. Hackworth operated on tight profit margins, relying on principles of honour and fair play in his business dealings, consistent with his Methodist background, to see him through. Hackworth believed that, provided he was given a decent specification, and estimates for manpower and materials which were reasonable, he could make a small profit on each engine produced. On the face of it there didn't seem to be a problem with the LBSCR deal, however the designer John Gray sang from a different hymn sheet from Hackworth. Gray was an inveterate tinkerer, constantly playing with his own designs and making costly and significant last-minute changes, sometimes just weeks before an engine was ready to roll off what constituted the production line. This caused unexpected and unpredictable delays in the manufacturing process; delays to which the LBSCR responded by issuing fines in accordance with the penalty clause written into the contract. Both Timothy Hackworth and eldest son John were soon semi-permanent residents of London, conducting protracted and evermore acrimonious meetings with the LBSCR management over perceived shortcomings in the Shildon engines. On one occasion, John Hackworth stormed out of a meeting vowing never to return, being only persuaded to re-enter the fray following a desperate plea for help from his father. Things got worse, if such were possible, after the retirement of Gray mid-contract, and the appointment by the LBSCR of two short-order replacements, each newcomer bringing his personal changes to the mix. It is a testament to Hackworth's patience and resilience that the order was ever completed at all. Tinkering seemed to be part and parcel of the way the LBSCR operated. Even after the engines entered service they were not left alone long to get on with their work. Modifications, and modifications on top of modifications, continued throughout the engines' 30-year working life such that by the end of their days, all the delivered locomotives had been effectively completely rebuilt, sometimes twice.

With regular work in short supply at Soho Works, and his designs seen as passé, Timothy made one last brave attempt to arouse interest. A show engine was built with the aim of demonstrating its potential. It was called *Sanspareil No.2*, after Hackworth's Rainhill locomotive, and incorporated all the best features of design Hackworth had assimilated in his forty years in the business. Intended for speedy passenger traffic, it was a sporty 2-2-2, in the manner of the recent LBSCR engines with a single pair of two metre diameter driving wheels and by the standards of the day it was indeed 'state of the art'. Unfortunately, nobody wanted to know about it. To spread the word Timothy arranged for *Sanspareil* to be trialled right across the country on any railway prepared to give it a chance, beginning with three spells on Hudson's York, Newcastle and Berwick Railway. Sales pitches were sent to all the major players of the day, each promotional flyer sounding more desperate than the last. In November 1849 for example, he wrote to Thomas Wrightly of the East Lancashire Railway:

'A few days ago I addressed a letter to John Robertson Kay esq. respecting a very superior Locomotive Engine I am bringing out. That gentleman having refered (sic) to you allow me to say I am now at liberty to offer to your inspection or any Railway Co. with whom you are contacted one of the best engines that has ever been produced.

No expense has been spared either in workmanship or materials and the experience of years has been brought to bear upon it. Whether it is viewed with regard to its manufacture construction or light consumption of coke it is generally admitted by competent judges to be without a parallel. A few experimental trips have been made on the York, Newcastle and Berwick Railway and it has been clearly proved that we have effected a saving of fully 25 per cent over the best Engines of the present days. I would here mention that the price of my Engine is £3000 to any Railway Company taking it with the promises I should have an order provided it accomplish what I have specified. This is I assure you a very great sacrifice but as I am anxious the improvements should be more fully known I willingly make it. For a good order my price per Engine would be £2500. I would just add I have had to do with the Locomotive from its first commencement a period of more than thirty-nine years and perhaps some of the most startling improvements in the Locomotive Engine have originated with me. Hoping to secure your influence on my behalf and beging the favour of a reply.'[38]

It is notable that Timothy was already prepared to drop the original asking price by £500.

John Hackworth accompanied the engine on its weary travels around the UK. He spent two weeks at Wolverton, the engineering centre of the London and North Western Railway, where the engine performed well; yet still Soho Works failed to secure an order. In desperation, John Hackworth issued a challenge to Robert Stephenson, offering to compete *Sanspareil No. 2* against the best that Forth Street could offer. Stephenson, unsurprisingly, ignored the contest. He had nothing to gain by meeting Hackworth's challenge. His reputation was already secure. Now seen as irrelevant in a cut-throat market, *Sanspareil* No. 2 found no takers anywhere and

Hackworth's final throw of the dice ended in failure. Within weeks of writing the letter above, Timothy was dead from typhus and so, effectively, was Soho Works. *Sanspareil No. 2* was the last gasp of a company well past its sell-by-date. The works and manufacturing equipment had had little investment in the previous decade and was dilapidated, antiquated and inefficient. It would have taken more money to bring the factory up to the standards of the opposition than its proprietor could ever recoup from the factory's output. Following Timothy's death, John Hackworth set up his own engineering business in Darlington. While Soho Works struggled along under the direction of Timothy's second son, also called Timothy. When the younger Timothy began struggling to cope with the business due to medical problems associated with diabetes, the Works was put up for sale. The wording of the sale advertisement was:

'The above Premises occupy a space of 9,608 square yards or thereabouts, and contain Engine Building Shed, Smiths' shop, Fitting Shop, Foundry, Store house, Pattern Shop, Office, Dwelling House and six well-built cottages, the whole enclosing a yard of large dimensions into which is laid a Branch Railway, connected with the main line of the Stockton and Darlington Railway.'

Offered separately to the buildings was:

'18,189 square yards of building ground, about half of which adjoins the property on the west side … The remaining portion is only severed from the above by a Colliery Branch Railroad'.[39]

There were no takers. Soho Works struggled on gamely for a couple more years. Timothy Hackworth Jnr. even tried making farm machinery, but the Works was just not profitable and was eventually sold for £4,900, half the original asking price, to the S&DR. The sale included an area of undeveloped land to the west which the S&DR immediately earmarked for the site of their gas works. The sale caused a rift in the family. Despite infirmity, Timothy Hackworth Jnr. wanted to continue his father's business and, as late as May 1852, he was still optimistic about the firm's prospects. His description of New Shildon in a letter dated 5 May to his sister Jenny bears recounting:

'I have just had a walk on the spoil bank for a few minutes; it is becoming quite a place of attraction, the men are now getting their gardens put in order and besides the Company have commenced making a reservoir on the top of the hill just opposite our works; we hope they do not mean to drown us out of the place. It is such a splendid afternoon; there are hundreds of people walking out in the fields around our City (*for 'City' read New Shildon*). It quite reminds me of the London parks on Sunday.'

A new reservoir was being built by the S&DR on the opposite side of the rails to Soho Cottage, on the north side of the Bishop Auckland line tunnel accommodation railway embankment. That the 'London parks' mentioned might laud the presence of a 'spoil bank' as 'quite a place of attraction' seems unlikely.

As Soho Works declined, the Shildon Works Company (SWC) prospered. There was no real pressure on the SWC to produce all the locomotives the S&DR needed since other manufacturers were now champing at the bit, desperate for business, crucially prepared, in the febrile financial climate of the day, to negotiate low-profit deals. During the 1840s, Kitching's factory at Darlington alone supplied thirteen S&DR engines including the 0-6-0 *Derwent*, which was built to Timothy Hackworth's design and is now to be seen at Darlington's 'Head of Steam' museum. Fifteen engines were also bought second-hand from other railways. Even, as stated, Hackworth's younger brother Thomas chipped in with an engine from his works at Stockton, which was a typical Hackworth 0-6-0 named 'Stockton'. With the pressure off, the time had come for the SWC to diversify.

The first flex of Shildon Works Company muscles in the winter of 1840 extended their output repertoire to the construction of passenger coaches for other railway companies. Railway carriages were to be produced at Shildon for the Great North of England Railway (GNOER); the customer's specification including the clause that all the carriages should be 'covered, if found preferable'. Whether or not their passengers' 'preference' was taken into consideration here seems debateable.[40] All locomotives, in the S&DR's massive and expanding fleet, however, still needed to be maintained, and as the antiquated machinery of Soho Works fell silent, the workshops of their near neighbours clamoured.

It is difficult to adequately quantify the contribution Timothy Hackworth made to the development of New Shildon. When he began working there, on what had been until recently marshland, the S&DR works consisted of a couple of primitive workshops and an open-sided car-port, where both locomotive assembly and maintenance was conducted. His legacy to the town was a booming industrial complex, which included a multi-unit engineering park covering hundreds of acres and employing thousands of local people. New Shildon owed its very existence to the railway and Timothy Hackworth was the railway Company's outstanding genius.

CHAPTER SEVEN

Shildon Works and the North Eastern Railway

Bouch's 0-6-0
Commerce, built 1847 (from a nineteenth century print).

Looking at images of the early locomotives from Shildon built to the design of William Bouch, as opposed to those of Timothy Hackworth, the obvious difference is in their appearance. I openly confess to not being an expert on locomotive engineering, so I cannot, hand on heart, say if there was any significant technical improvement over the earlier Hackworth engines, but simply in terms of how they look, the Bouch engines win hands down. With their sleek Robert Stephenson style long-boilers and a superstructure unencumbered by external pipework or Hackworth's sloping cylinders, Bouch's engines look much as steam locos do today. However, the six Shildon class engines, built immediately after Bouch and Gilkes took over the reins were, unsurprisingly, similar in construction to the Hackworth engines that went before. The first true Bouch engine to emerge was *Meteor*, a handsome 2-2-2 passenger loco. This was followed by Bouch's three Commerce class 0-6-0 freight locos, which, other than the lack of a cab for the poor driver, to my eyes just look 'modern'. The Stephenson influence is obvious from the start. Bouch had served his apprenticeship at Forth Street, before moving to Butterley Iron Works as their resident engineer and during his time at Newcastle Bouch can't fail to have noted the mechanical improvements Robert Stephenson was introducing. On appointment at Shildon, Bouch began the process of sweeping away everything that went before. Since he wasn't a New Shildon man, he had no filial commitment to the town and it came as no surprise when he eventually oversaw the transfer of locomotive production from Shildon to Darlington, which then became his home. Nevertheless, this was a gradual process with an extended transitional period. For many years locomotive manufacture continued as before. Although it is difficult to identify exactly which locomotives were built at Shildon Works once the Company became part of the NER empire, since some were merely 'assemblies', the occasional locomotive was still being built from scratch there as late as 1870. The committee report for 19 January 1870 states:

'That the Shildon Works Company be authorised to proceed during the current half year with the construction of four new locomotive engines *in addition to those now in progress*.' (my italics)

Locomotive production at Shildon was obviously still 'in progress' in 1870, but which NER engines were under construction isn't obvious from the records, although there are many candidates in the company's records, for whom the original home of manufacture is unclear.

In truth, however, by the end of the sixties production of railway locomotives at Shildon was just a side-line. This move away from loco production had its origin in events which occurred a decade earlier, at a time when Bouch was having major problems finding sufficient freight wagons to fulfil his customers' demands.

A surge in requests for coal wagons, during the summer of 1844, was the ultimate motivation the company needed to bring wagon production in-house. Barely had the Company released 200 wagons out to customers when a further 200 were requested. With no part of the works dedicated to wagon production, they had to be sourced elsewhere. Times were desperate, and any supplier would do. Of the firms willing to quote, perhaps the most surprising was Fossick and Hackworth (F&H) who duly provided 100 trucks. F&H was the Works part-owned by Thomas Hackworth at Stockton. His company only existed as a result of Thomas's rancorous exit from the managerial position at Soho Works where, it may be recalled, his departure had resulted from repeated S&DR complaints about the quality of the work delivered by Hackworth and Downing, and its successor Thomas Hackworth and Co. Now, it seemed the SWC were prepared to let bygones be bygones. There is even a reference to the acquisition of a locomotive from 'Fossick and Hackworth', in

in Station Street, where a concert was provided, attended by more than 500 people, in a hall designed for 350. Oversubscription seems to have been a feature of Shildon celebrations. Temperance restrictions meant that the drinking of alcohol at the Railway Institute was forbidden, as was smoking. Even participation in recreational games was restricted to the playing of draughts. This was a smart move since a subsequent reversal of the decision, which permitted card-playing on the premises, led to debauchery on an unprecedented scale:

'The privilege of being allowed to play games with cards was abused on various occasions by certain members who ignored the objects for which the institute existed and surreptitiously used the recreation room for the purpose of gambling.'

The Institute decree doesn't indicate whether pocket watch and frying pan competitions were deemed acceptable.

For thirty years, the S&DR had been top-dog in the North East, having by far the most extensive rail network. Bit by bit, however, and driven mostly by the ambition of the much-maligned George Hudson, most of the other companies in the North-East were slowly absorbed into Hudson's empire which had now become a formidable opposition. Unfortunately, at the time when Hudson should have been celebrating his position as supremo of all the major northern railways, he lost everything he had acquired through dodgy dealings, and the main beneficiary was the NER. By the end of the 1860s therefore, it was the NER which was the major player and a merger between the two largest railway companies, the NER and S&DR, seemed inevitable. This created the lip-smacking prospect for shareholders of having all the lucrative rail routes in the North East, coast to coast, under one roof. In 1860, the NER made an initial overture to the S&DR, offering generous terms for a merger. This wasn't popular with the other railways in the region, particularly the West Hartlepool Dock and Harbour Company, fronted by the West Hartlepool based mini-empire builder Ralph Ward Jackson, whose company had absorbed the S&DR's former nemesis, the Clarence Railway. Jackson was one of the main objectors to the 1863 merger bill.

Rather than inflict damage on future NER partners, negotiations temporarily paused. Three years later however the climate had improved, and in July 1863 the S&DR finally became part of the NER. This pioneering railway, the S&DR, essentially the birthplace of modern railways, was no more. However, if unequal partners in the deal, the network and infrastructure of the S&DR was allowed to continue undisturbed for a period of ten years. During that decade, what had once been the S&DR operated as before, with the same infrastructure and staff.[43] All the existing workshops, rolling stock, etc. were retained, so in the short term the public would hardly have noted any change. At Shildon, William Bouch continued to design and build engines as before, although it was now inevitable that locomotive production would move to new workshops under construction at Darlington. A move to Darlo had been considered long before the NER appeared on the scene. The first step in the transition was to transfer (at least nominally) loco repair work, whereupon the former locomotive maintenance building at Shildon would become a wagon repair shop. Some minor locomotive maintenance work would continue at New Shildon dependent on workshop availability at Darlington. This back-up role would continue. As late as September 1907 repairs to locomotives were still being carried out at Shildon, however, customer requests for

Inside the wagon repair shop (picture courtesy Locomotion).

wagons were now at record levels. In 1870 alone, 2,000 new trucks were requested by S&DR customers, 1,000 of which were solely dedicated to construction work for blast furnaces at Middlesbrough.

If Darlington was now the company's maternity ward for locomotives, New Shildon was still the focal point for freight activity, particularly in respect of the core business of coal traffic. The town had now developed beyond recognition. Everywhere there was the clash and clang of machinery with an atmosphere choked by smoke from a dozen belching chimneys. Within an area of under two square miles, New Shildon boasted an industrial gas works, a working coal mine and one of the biggest railway works in the world, all interwoven with row on row of back-to-back terraced houses, for the miners and railwaymen that manned the industry. As contemporary reports make clear it was far from pretty. Dickens' description of Camden in the middle of the nineteenth century could equally have applied to Victorian New Shildon:

'Everywhere there were bridges that led nowhere; thoroughfares that were wholly impassable; Babel towers of chimneys, wanting half their height; temporary wooden houses and enclosures, in the most unlikely situations; carcases of ragged tenements and fragments of unfinished walls and arches, and piles of scaffolding, and wildernesses of bricks, and giant forms of cranes and tripods straddling above nothing. There were a hundred thousand shapes and substances of incompleteness, wildly mingled out of their places, upside down, burrowing in the earth, aspiring in the air, mouldering in the water, and unintelligible as any dream… Boiling water hissed and heaved within dilapidated walls; whence, also, the glare and roar of flames came issuing forth; and mounds of ashes blocked up rights of way, and wholly changed the law and custom of the neighbourhood.'[44]

Amidst all this chaos, plans were being made to extend the Company's already extensive marshalling yard, where incoming coal and mineral trains from the surrounding area were sorted and aggregated for transfer to destinations throughout the country. Shildon yard had become the biggest and busiest in the land and the 24-hour rattle and bang of shunting wagons kept light sleepers in the town awake for a further century. The yard extended over sixteen acres and boasted more than ten miles of track, virtually all of which was managed without additional motive support from

Shildon marshalling yard, c.1900 (from a nineteenth century postcard).

steam locomotives.[45] The principle of gravity marshalling, whereby loaded wagons are sorted into sidings using a falling gradient, was long established. It had been around in one form or another almost from the beginning of railways but would achieve its most impressive incarnation at Shildon where continuous lines of trucks could be seen every day trundling along from one part of the yard to the other without obvious propulsive power. Despite health and safety concerns, the speed of the wagons was controlled by a brakesman, who stood on the buffers at the rear end of the trucks. He adjusted the speed by careful application of his hand brake, a practice which dated from the earliest days of the S&DR. Needless to say, this was a regular cause of accidents.

In May 1904, a brakesman, Samuel Brown, was handling the descent of ten loaded wagons into the Shildon marshalling yards. Applying the handbrake, he slowed the wagons to a crawl but was unable to fully bring them to a stop. In panic he jumped down from his perch and ran alongside the moving waggons, unsure of what to do next. If he had been fitter, he could have boarded a passing wagon and applied the brake, but he panicked and, grabbing a length of timber from the trackside, thrust it between the spokes of the nearest wheel. The timber along with Brown's hand was dragged into the spokes and mangled. This unpleasant incident, however, was eclipsed by another at the same location earlier that year. In March, a 20-year-old Assistant Shunter called John Wilson was running the gauntlet between rows of slowly moving wagons, trying to aggregate groups of trucks for onward transport. This practice was officially forbidden but had nevertheless become common practice. It was late in the day, 11pm, and in attempting to dodge between the wagons Wilson's luck finally ran out and he was crushed between two loaded trucks.[46] 1904 was a bad year for Shildon. Another man, Christopher Brownless, was killed a few weeks later and his colleague badly injured when two tons of unsecured logs rolled off a wagon, crushing them both.

Accidents were inevitable in the Shildon yard. It was a dynamic place. Its size and efficiency were attracting world-wide attention, to the point it was the main discussion topic of the 3rd International Railway Conference, held in Paris in 1889. Details of how the yard could handle such a huge tonnage of minerals every day was marvelled at by railwaymen from around the globe.[47] It is interesting to speculate therefore how many marshalling yards across the globe are based on the Shildon model.

Virtually none of the Shildon yard has survived. One section, however, now houses the impressive glass and metal Large Collection Building of Locomotion. In its heyday most of the wagons being shunted in the marshalling yard were also built at Shildon. It might be an opportune moment therefore for the Wagon Works to have its own chapter.

Chapter Eight

Shildon Wagon Works

Late 1970s, aerial view of Shildon Wagon Works (BREL publicity picture).

As Shildon turned its back on locomotive production, local focus shifted to freight wagons, and this branch of railway business became the main reason for the town's existence over the next hundred years. In the years immediately prior to closure there were 2750 people employed in the wagon works alone.

Initially, all wagons used by the S&DR, as already noted, were purchased externally and even as late as the turn of the century specialist wagons were being purchased elsewhere. All the wagons used for lime transport, for example, which had to be lined with heat resistant material, because the lime was hot when loaded, did not lend themselves to mass production and were better outsourced. Even after the creation of an additional wagon manufactory at

Darlington, towards the end of the nineteenth century, the NER were still purchasing wagons from other manufacturers.

The Shildon wagons at the beginning were used both by the Company itself and also loaned out to the many independent operators who leased time on the rails at the typical rate of four pence/ton/mile. These primitive wagons, or chaldrons, as illustrated on the Company seal, were wooden-sided affairs with spoked cast-iron wheels of the type favoured by collieries, and designed to accommodate a maximum of 3 tons.

The company's wagons were painted grey or black, with the title 'S & DR' spelled out in white on the sides; one of the originals can be seen on a plinth in Old Shildon near the site of the former Phoenix Foundry.

When the young Prussian engineers visited Shildon, in the spring of 1827, all these wagons were reported as having been purchased elsewhere at a cost between £24 and £28. The two men were scathing about the fragility of their cast-iron wheels. In consequence, one of the earliest activities seen to be undertaken

Early S&DR chaldron wagon on a plinth in Old Shildon.

at New Shildon was wagon repairs, which were conducted in the rudimentary workshops. This situation continued right through the 1830s and '40s, with wagons bought externally and maintained at Shildon. It was only in 1840, when New Shildon Works came under the control of Gilkes and Bouch, that an effort was made to ensure most wagons were made in-house. A conscious decision to divert effort from locomotive to wagon production is apparent in the earliest logs and committee minutes. The S&DR owned company that Gilkes and Bouch took over became officially known as the 'Shildon Works Company'. The S&DR had used 'Shildon Works' as an informal name prior to this date, with reference to their own site immediately to the east of Brusselton incline but until the establishment of Shildon Works Co, in 1840, it previously had no legal recognition.

The lack of available wagons had been a sore point for years, but things came to a head in 1847 when there were a series of complaints that wagons loaned to customers for S&DR work were being appropriated by friends and neighbours of their customers for their own internal use. Turnaround was the big issue. Wagons were often loaded and offloaded by hand, and where goods needed delicate handling, the time factor increased accordingly; the loading of one wagon with building tiles, for example, was reported as taking four days.[48] The need for a readily available stock of reliable wagons had never been so acute. There were at one time upwards of 300 wagons just awaiting repair. A change of direction is clear in committee minutes from January 1847:

> 'Resolved that in consequence of the above (400) applications, the managers are desired to keep up the number of common wagons and to proceed with the making of them themselves, having special reference to the experience already obtained as to the quality of the wheels and report to the next committee at what rate they can make them.'

Despite the implication that wheels would now be forged at SWW, for many years the production of most moving parts including axles and wheels was outsourced, to companies such as Fossick and Hackworth at Stockton, and the components merely fitted to wagon bodies at Shildon. However, from 1847 onwards and wherever possible, all forging, welding and assembly work was meant to be conducted at the SWC. To achieve this, a dedicated wagon unit was needed and this required a comprehensive makeover of the works. Routine maintenance of wagons continued as before but was transferred to another building nearby. Given the enthusiasm for change, it took another seven years before a suitably kitted out wagon shop was up and running. Its construction coincided with overall control passing from the S&DR to the NER. From then on, wagon manufacture and maintenance were the main reason for SWC's existence. The move to wagon production was never a smooth transition. Shildon continued to deputise for Darlington whenever locomotive manufacture and maintenance exceeded plant or manpower capacity over at North Road Works. Six new locomotives, for example, were built by the NER at Shildon during the 1860s, the heavy freight 0-6-0s *Gladstone, Barrow, London, John Dixon, Ireland and England*.

General railway support activities continued in one form or another during the same period. As late as 1871, New Shildon was still viewed as the main support centre for the Railway. Nevertheless, wagon manufacture and maintenance had now assumed pride of place. In that year, alone the works repaired 6,700 engines, 54,000 wagons and 34,000 trucks, and manufactured 600 new wagons.[49] The railway remained the main employer in the expanding town. The census for 1881 showed that every house in Station Street, East Thickley, was occupied by railwaymen; mostly engine fireman or drivers, including John Glass who was now the Company's Shildon Works Clerk (by then Shildon and New Shildon had become one town). With the noise and smoke from the SWW, working flat out, and the recent appearance of new collieries right in the centre of the town, Shildon was not an attractive place to live. In fact the *Northern Echo* claimed it to be 'one of the ugliest places on the earth's fair planet'. Shildon in the 1870s is described in the local newspaper as follows:

'It is now a hideous congerie (*a congerie is a 'disorderly, mass, heap'*
according to the 'Concise Oxford Dictionary') of houses, growing like
fungus on either side of a network of rails. A huge colliery rears its
ungainly head close to the rails and the noise of its working ceases
not for ever. Engines are plying about with reckless activity,
like spiders running around the threads of their nets seeking
for hapless flies. There is a ceaseless rattle of wagon wheels and
snorting and puffing of the engines fills the air with dismal noises,
as if locomotives were sentient beings and the hospital was filled
with the sound of their groanings.'

It seems likely the writer of the piece had been raised in more genteel environments than those which now surrounded him. The average locomotive buff, and I include myself here, might have viewed the landscape differently.

Shildon station (from a postcard dating from the turn of the twentieth century) with the same view today. Which is better? You decide.

Not content with bad-mouthing the town, the same journalist then turned his attention to Shildon station which was little different to the cobbled-together compromise of the 1840s:

'Shildon Station is a disgrace to Durham, to the Stockton and Darlington and to the railway system. The booking office is a shanty perched on the top of a high bank entirely disconnected from the low lying draughty sheds, which are supposed to shelter the passengers who have the ill-luck to alight on its platforms. Perhaps this wretched apology for a station is continued in existence as a memento of the past.'

Even so, most local people had steady work; families were raised, general health improved, and life expectancy grew year on year. By the middle of the seventies, however, the Works had stopped manufacturing steam locomotives although it was still the first port of call after Darlington in terms of engine assembly and maintenance. How many locomotives were assembled there during this decade isn't clear, but it wasn't until the 1890s before locomotive maintenance work could be said to have ceased completely. According to Lowe, for example, four locomotives were assembled at Shildon in 1865, (0-6-0s *Spring, Summer, Alice* and *Helena*).

The cessation was accompanied by the construction of a new smiths shop, additional forges, a machine shop, sawmill – and crucially, a new purpose-built wagon shop, which opened in 1897. From that year, the former railway support works could finally be thought of as purely a wagon works namely (the Shildon Wagon Works (SWW)). The final obvious steam locomotive link to the town was severed in 1935, when the LNER closed Shildon engine shed and moved most of the resident locos to West Auckland. The terms 'Wagon Works' and 'Shildon', however, were now synonymous. The Works itself had expanded beyond all expectations. By the time it became absorbed into the nationalised British Railways, it could boast a forge, wagon building shop, paint shop, axle-box shop, smiths shop, machine shop, frame welding shop, body building shop, a separate paint shop for welded wagons and a wagon repair unit with its own sawmill. The latter utilised the buildings which formerly housed steam locomotives, suitably modified by the addition of travelling cranes for moving heavy equipment around.

Needless to say remnants of the old works buildings can still be found, blended into the factories that now occupy the Hackworth Industrial Estate.

Surviving part of the Wagon Works Lift and Brake Shop, now units on the Hackworth Industrial Estate.

Even though the Works could claim to be the best in the world, it was not all plain sailing in terms of its financial viability. The decade prior to the Second World War was a low point in terms of output. The malaise of the depression years had slaked the nation's thirst for coal. This, in turn, caused a downturn in the national need for freight rolling stock, such that in the year preceding the Second World War less than one wagon was being made at Shildon in any one week.[50] The converse, of course, was that during the two world wars it was boom-time for such industry.

The war years brought about change. Female staff had to be recruited to replace conscripted (and volunteer) male employees who left to do their bit for King and Country. In the words of former employee, R. Spedding, who was apprenticed in 1940 and retired just before the closure of the works in 1984:

'At first the women were a source of amusement and thought incapable of doing the heavy work expected of them. But they proved their critics wrong. They were extremely tough and capable and played a vital role in the war effort. They were eventually employed in most jobs, from sweeping the shop floors to wheeling heavy laden barrows, but perhaps the most surprising was to find them employed in the heat, noise and dirt of the forge and smiths shop. Some even operated the heavy drop-hammers, a job considered rough and undesirable by any standard.'

There were unexpected bonuses to be had from the women's presence. There was suddenly a requirement for better sanitary hygiene. As Spedding put it:

'Previously washing one's hands was frowned upon and facilities were primitive. They consisted of battered tins or buckets, each

Women volunteers at Shildon Works during the First World War. The locomotive in the picture is 0-8-0 Q5 444, later BR 63295 (from a wartime NER publicity photograph, courtesy of Beamish Museum).

jealously guarded by four or five men, representing a group or unit. There were hundreds of these groups or units scattered throughout the factory. The men would take turns to go to the smiths shop or forge and return with a piece of red hot steel or iron. This was dropped into the tin or bucket containing cold water, and, hey presto – hot water 'For the use of…'[51]

The improvements resulting from the ladies' presence extended to the loos:

'The early toilets were also communal and very unhygienic by today's standards. The seating consisted of one long plank running the length of the building and divided into eight cubicles, each one partitioned and accommodation for one person. The water channel also ran the full length of the building and carried the water below the seating in a continual flow.'

Prior to the employment of women, a regular laddish jape was to make a paper boat out of an old newspaper, set fire to it and then float it in the water channel that ran downstream beneath the toilet cubicles – to the general hilarity of all, except perhaps the occupants. Such antics, benignly tolerated by the management, were no longer considered appropriate for a mixed workforce. New toilet and washing facilities were therefore provided which would eventually outlive the presence of the female employees, who were laid off at the end of both wars to accommodate returning servicemen.

The SWW, considering its undoubted military significance, was fortunate in never being hit by German bombs. The engineering nature of the work made Shildon Works an obvious target for the Luftwaffe. During the Second World War, crude air raid shelters were therefore excavated for the workers, in the land between the Works and the Brusselton incline. The marshy origins of the land now showed its face. Young apprentices were tasked with digging the shelters and this was no easy undertaking. The excavations made for the subsurface Nissen huts continually filled with water, which needed to be pumped away by hand, making them virtually impossible to use at short notice. At best it would have been a damp way of avoiding air raids. Luckily, whilst the coastal towns in the North-East were heavily bombed, Shildon, at the heart of rural Durham, escaped and the shelters were never needed. There were near misses of course. The old town at the top of the shield was hit, and both British and German planes crashed on high ground nearby, yet somehow the Works emerged from both wars unscathed. In fact, the only tangible effect on the Wagon Works during the Second World War, apart from the unprecedented use of female labour and MOD imposed changes to manufacturing output, was an influx of Italian prisoners-of-war. The POWs were recruited from a nearby camp and were willing to find any alternative to the confinement and boredom of prison. Unlike their German counterparts, the Italians were more than happy to be a long way away from the ongoing conflict and, by the end of the war, they were sufficiently trusted to be permitted to drive shunting engines, both in the Works and in the nearby marshalling yard.[52] In the years immediately preceding the war, the Works had taken no part in the maintenance of locomotives. However, during the war years, steam locomotives were once again serviced at Shildon, since it was a less obvious target for bombers than Darlington, a town easily identifiable on the main line between London and Edinburgh. Despite this, the core side of the business continued apace. Nearly 10,000 new wagons were made at Shildon between 1939 and 1945, along with repairs to 43,000 wagons. MOD-related activities also become part of daily routine with the Works turning out heavy gun parts, forging the bodies of gun carriages, forging tank tracks and producing sections of the temporary bridges eventually used by the army in the aftermath of the Normandy landings.[53]

Over the years, the Works created its own emergency service infrastructure. It even possessed a fire engine with a trained crew. Originally horse-drawn, this, for many years, was mounted on a wagon and moved around by a locomotive. In its final, conventional, motorised incarnation it was never used in anger at the Works. Nevertheless, it did see brief active service when it was co-opted by the Durham County Fire Brigade to support the many machines deployed at West Hartlepool docks during the Match Factory fire of August 1954; a fire which coincidentally threatened to engulf the adjacent Middlesbrough to Sunderland railway line. Despite the presence of forges and furnaces, fires at the Works were, surprisingly, rare events. Dust explosions, however, were commonplace. Spedding reported an incident in which he was nearly killed by just such an incident in the Attritor House, where the conveyor, which fed pulverised fuel to the works, was located. For a couple of years, pulverised coal dust (PCD), which was cheap and locally abundant, was trialled as a fuel for the furnaces.

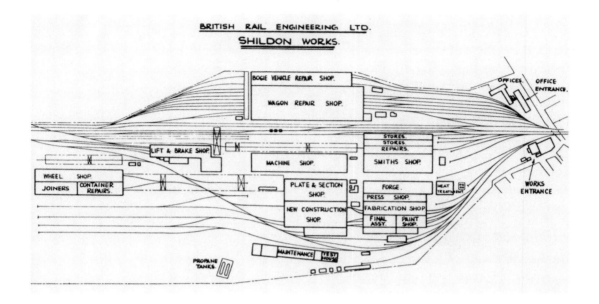

BRITISH RAIL ENGINEERING LTD.
SHILDON WORKS.

Plan of Shildon Wagon Works in its 1970 BREL days (from a BREL promotional leaflet).

The PCD was stored in a cyclone which Spedding was expected to repair whenever it malfunctioned. During a routine inspection he and a young colleague removed the cyclone cover whereupon a cloud of dust flowed out and over a small gas-fired pre-heater. The resulting explosion shook the Works and threatened to hurl the men from their perilous perch high on top of the cyclone. This would certainly have killed them but somehow they clung on and escaped without injury, nevertheless sporting black faces, missing hair and eyebrows and serious loss of dignity. Use of PCD as a fuel was subsequently deemed a failure and the idea abandoned. This would doubtless have pleased the population of Shildon, as the dust, which lay on every surface of the plant, also floated beyond the boundary of the Works to settle on fresh lines of washing.[54]

Concentrating their effort on wagon production meant that the Company could now improvise and specialise. And what wagons the workforce produced; a world removed from the half-timbered supermarket trolley lookalikes the S&DR had once used to move coal. The new wave of wagons was also industry specific. Watertight wagons were manufactured for the cement industry, flat-beds for the car industry and the armed forces, tankers for handling liquids and powders in bulk, and specialist 'carousel' coal wagons that could load and offload coal without ever having to stop. These wagons were much favoured by the Central Electricity Generating Board (CEGB). The wagons loaded and unloaded automatically on circular turnaround tracks. Hence the name. The last of the carousel wagons was purchased by the 'Friends of the NRM' and is now housed at Locomotion.

Products of Shildon Wagon Works.

All were beautiful, sleek, and so massive they would have dwarfed any vehicle in the original S&DR rolling stock, including its locomotives. The marshalling yard at times was crowded with rows of freshly painted wagons decked out in all the colours of the rainbow. Wagons were produced in such numbers that it is now impossible to avoid seeing Shildon Wagon Works plates on any railway memorabilia stall and now one of the first sights to greet visitors to Locomotion is the former SWW wagons lined up near the entrance. An appropriate location since the museum was built on the site of the extensive marshalling yard.

It is hard to comprehend, therefore, how such a national treasure could so easily be destroyed. As late as June 1964, British Railways were vaunting a £17 million modernisation plan for the Works with a further million pounds to be provided the following year to 'stabilise the workforce' at 2,300. But the Wagon Works days were numbered.[55]

Not long before the end, however, there was one final dramatic swansong. In 1975, in preparation for a locomotive parade

from New Shildon to Heighington, to commemorate the 150th anniversary of the S&DR, the wagon repair shop and adjacent yard were temporarily cleared to house the 35 locomotives recruited to participate in the cavalcade. Since the repair shop had been Shildon's engine shed, this was an appropriate tribute to the glory days. In the weeks leading up to the event normal work was put on hold, while British Rail pulled out all the stops to ensure everything went well. Locomotives arriving at Shildon in poor condition were taken into the Works and given a facelift, with the engineering shops suitably tooled up to provide the support needed for such an important national event. Work conducted at the Works in support of the big day was not necessarily railway related. It included, for example, the manufacture of the temporary crowd control safety barriers fitted alongside the track. The return of steam to Shildon stirred something in the local DNA. As Spedding described it:

'When the steam engines arrived at Shildon shops the whole atmosphere seemed to change. It took on an air of expectation,

The Shildon produced NCB 'carousel' coal wagon, purchased by the Friends of the NRM, at Locomotion.

rules and regulations were relaxed and going to work was no longer looked upon as a daily exercise but an exciting privilege.'

The parade of world famous engines was fronted by a replica of Stephenson's *Locomotion No. 1*, fitted with a petrol engine, but producing a plume of convincing looking smoke. The attached tender and carriage was more authentic since it dated from the final years of the S&DR. The carriage, nevertheless, had to be rebuilt by the technicians of the SWW, a fitting farewell to the railway heritage of New Shildon.

CHAPTER NINE

Industrial Unrest

Not surprisingly it wasn't always sweetness and light on the shop floor. Shildon men were not famous for forelock touching and no respecters of authority. Timothy Hackworth was once asked by the S&DR to intervene to protect a railway policeman who had been subjected to daily threats from the Shildon workforce while attempting to do his job.[56] Workmates were not immune. It was reported that one driver took umbrage at his colleague's disinterest and focused his attention by hitting hit him on the head with a club hammer.[57] The Company's employees were tough cookies. In consequence, the NER, particularly, always had a fractious relationship with their staff. The introduction of unwanted and much resented work

Soldiers guarding the marshalling yard at Shildon during the industrial action of 1911 (picture courtesy of Beamish Industrial Museum).

conditions in the autumn of 1899 produced industrial unrest on an unprecedented scale. This led to the wholesale adoption of trade union membership at the Wagon Works, which the management can't have counted upon. The causes of unrest were manifold, but low rates of pay and long hours were the main reason for complaints. The men were unquestionably poorly paid. From manual labourers to the technically skilled, wages were low compared with their counterparts on other railways. According to the *Northern Echo*, 'labourers with families received 17 shillings a week. Men who had served their time at the works received only 18s or 19s a week, while the wage of a skilled artisan was merely 23s per week.'

If that wasn't enough, Shildon rates of pay were the worst within the NER itself. Matters came to a head following the imposition of new and even more onerous working conditions without prior consultation with the men affected. The existing working day had been from 6am to 5pm but the NER now expected the men to work right through to 9pm without notice, if instructed to do so. Additionally, anyone arriving late on a Monday forfeited the right to work the lucrative half-day Saturday, for which 'double time' was paid. There was no quid-pro-quo in this, management word was law. It had ever been ever so. Working conditions had barely improved in the thirty years of NER control. The only surprising thing was that the workforce had not rebelled sooner. The men's first step was the appointment of a committee, taking three representatives from each of the eight Works' departments. The committee was elected to represent the interests of 800 union members. Which trade union this would be, however, had yet to be determined. On 13 September, a mass meeting was held after work in a field just outside the Works' boundary. Representatives from the Steel Workers Union and General Railway Workers Union arrived to give promotional speeches extolling the benefits of trade union membership and each speaker was enthusiastically applauded. Change, it seems, was on the way.

Disputes between railwaymen and management at New Shildon were not new. During the two-year period of S&DR construction, in the 1820s, Company reports show that work regularly came to a halt because of management/workforce disagreements. These disputes, however, usually involved one or two individuals arguing over a single issue, such as pay inequality, with their employer. Such one-sided David v Goliath confrontations always ended in favour of the management since, holding all the cards, it could hire and fire at will and often did. Contracts, such as there were, were always couched in favour of the employer. The management could even reduce wages whenever it felt like it without any consultation whatsoever. This usually happened whenever the Company saw a downturn in profits. Staff wages, for example, were arbitrarily reduced in the years 1830, 1833, 1842, 1848 and 1857.[58] Since these alterations in terms and conditions were made in the Company's own words 'without reference to the men' we do not know the reasons behind them. Most likely, the cause of wage reduction resulted from market force fluctuations, but it could also have been caused by a glut of available labour. There was rarely any problem finding unskilled labour at Shildon. Manual railway work was considered less demanding than either agricultural work or coal mining which were the other local alternatives on offer. The harsh economics of the market place particularly affected the poorly educated component of the workforce. As the years went by, the employer/ employee balance began to change. Following the merger of lots of small railway companies, there was a consequent increase in the numbers of men employed within a single organisation. The threat of industrial action from a significant percentage of the workforce now carried more weight. More importantly, the introduction of trade unions raised the possibility of collective action, which strengthened the workers' hand and made it more difficult for employers to resolve disagreements just by sacking those involved. It seems surprising therefore that, for whatever reason, railwaymen were amongst the last of the major engineering industries to fully embrace trade unionism. The late move to collective bargaining at Shildon had been typical of other railway employees throughout the land. According to the Oxford economist and historian Harold Pollins, the reluctance of workers to join trade unions in the railway industry was because:

'...the bulk of the labour was unskilled. The skilled men, the footplate crews were in general well looked after by the companies and had little in common with other railway employees.'

In other words, the companies controlled the workforce using a principle of divide and conquer. Only technically able and educated men needed to be 'looked after', although it could be argued in Shildon, that even this 'rule' was open to liberal interpretation. Footplatemen had taken industrial action in support of reduced hours and increased pay two years before. In 1867, unionised drivers and firemen downed tools for better pay and conditions. They received a short sharp shock. The minutes of the Company Works Committee for 24 April reported:

> 'Since the last meeting of the committee, viz on the 11th inst. 1,155 Drivers and 244 firemen and guards struck work without either notice or complaint but simply in obedience to the orders of the Union; this committee observes with much satisfaction that through the very efficient and successful efforts of Messrs. Bouch and Dale and other officers of the Co, but comparatively little inconvenience has been the result and that *there is now every prospect of the Company being well served by non-Union men'*. (my italics)

Before the Company attempted to make good on this unveiled threat, there were further rewards for those Union railwaymen who had defied the callout and to non-Union employees, now identified as future replacements for the 'disloyal' strikers.[59] One-off payments were made to former footplatemen who stepped into the breach and in a worrying move, which would be repeated in future similar disputes, inexperienced and downright inappropriate employees deputised whenever technically qualified railwaymen were unavailable:

> 'To men engaged (previous to the strike) in Departments or in services from which Engine Drivers would not in ordinary circumstances be selected, who acted as Drivers during the strike and have remained in that capacity £1 each.'

Lack of experience it seems was not a handicap when it came to the serious business of strike breaking:

> 'To men who rendered assistance as conductors or by acting as firemen, etc. £1 each *and to a number of youths and platelayers who were similarly engaged 10/- each.'* (my italics)

Given it was the unskilled majority who suffered most when it came to poor workplace pay and conditions, therefore it is ironic that the first trade union to take industrial action nationally was one which represented the interests of the better qualified and experienced railwaymen, namely the Engine Drivers and Firemen's United Society (EDFUS). In 1869, this newly formed union argued for a ten-hour working day, not least because serious accidents were becoming regular events due to drivers' working long hours. Having negotiated agreements with most of the railway companies throughout the land, the union reached an impasse with both the NER and the London, Brighton and South Coast Railway (LBSCR). Under duress, the NER agreed to a maximum twelve-hour working day but only if their employees would also agree to work unspecified and unpaid overtime. This provoked the predictable response. On 11 April 1869 more than 1,000 railwaymen in the NER came out on strike. In response, the Company brought in blackleg labour and instituted legal proceedings against the strike leaders claiming breach of contract. EDFUS hadn't the resources for a prolonged fight and the 1869 strike petered out, with the union itself folding a few weeks later.

Typical of the attitude taken by management was the dispute between the NER and one of its Shildon guards, George Staley, in January 1894. George was a prominent ASRS union member.[60] Not afraid to speak his mind on behalf of colleagues, he spoke up against the management's decision to impose a rigorous eye test on their frontline staff. This was perceived as just a ruse to edge out the older and hence better paid members of the Company's workforce. In sharp contrast to George Graham's experience in working long hours mentioned earlier, Staley was ordered to cease work after eight hours and take cheap lodgings near Normanton where his train terminated. Instead he chose to return to Shildon later the same day acting as the guard on the same train and therefore getting paid for his time. He was suspended from duty. Significantly, the driver and fireman who drove the train in both directions were not so disciplined. Union protests, marches and demonstrations in favour of Staley's reinstatement made no difference and Staley eventually left and became a coalman.[61]

By the turn of the century, walkouts in railway companies were commonplace to the point that the government established a Royal Commission, the sole object of which was to achieve a nationally agreed position on railwaymen's terms and conditions. These would be referred to in any negotiations between management and unions, along with an agreed procedure for mediation should there still be a dispute. The government's principal recommendation, however, was that before industrial action could be initiated by a trade union, the bone of contention had to be referred to an 'independent' arbitration board who would discuss the men's grievances with a panel consisting of the employer and unspecified government representatives. Predictably, the unions would not be involved in these discussions despite the outcome being binding upon them. Like most such agreements it was a fudge, doomed to failure because the Company representatives, particularly those of the NER, refused to negotiate directly with the trade unions. It is fair to say that railwaymen at the beginning of the twentieth century had lots to have grievances about. The average railwaymen's lot is neatly summarised in a poem titled 'Eighteen Bob a Week' which appeared in the 1911 November edition of the *Railway Gazette*. This contained the following lines, aimed directly at the employers:

'To them of course it is quite just to draw a princely ration
While we must get our grub on trust and slave at some dull station
Be bullied here and bullied there and take it all quite meek
To drive away all earthly care with eighteen bob a week.'

A weekly wage of eighteen shillings shows how little railwaymen's salaries had improved since 1899 and, for once, railwaymen were united. A national rail strike ensued and the day after strike action began the magazine *Railway Review* reported that in everywhere apart from London the walk-out was solid.

In those towns and cities across the country where union membership was strongest, such as Shildon, industrial action was also militant. Both sides refused to talk to each other and public safety was relegated to a secondary consideration. Most signalmen were union members and therefore subject to the Union walkout. Unfortunately for the management, signal operation was a technically complex operation requiring training over many years and didn't easily lend itself to blackleg intervention. Since temporary signalmen could not be found at short notice, many signal boxes during the dispute were therefore left unmanned. Daily scheduling was consequently reduced to maximise the time interval between trains and thus avoid collisions. Train drivers were easier to replace, although the quality of the replacements was often questionable. Many of the blackleg drivers brought in to break the unions had previously been dismissed by the same railway companies for misdemeanours, some indeed having failed to meet the most basic of competency assessments, including those related to health. Worryingly, health deficiencies included the inability to see. Amongst the blackleg drivers employed at Shildon, for example, was a man who had previously been dismissed because of defective eyesight. Since most signal boxes wouldn't be manned during the dispute, the requirement for a driver to respond to danger signals was presumably no longer considered vital.

With a generally belligerent workforce it was inevitable that Shildon would be one of the places where violent confrontations took place, and of all the stories concerning the strike none is more fascinating or bizarre than that relating to the face-off in 1911 between Shildon Station Master, Christopher Churchman, and his work colleagues. The menfolk of Shildon, as mentioned, were not famous for tolerance or sobriety. As Shildon historian Robert Corkin put it:

> 'There is no doubt that alcohol played a major role in the troubles that plagued Shildon. Engine drivers and fireman seemed to spend every penny they possessed on ale, then after 'a belly full' plan a full scale battle with the police or with anyone who tread their path'.[62]

It was unfortunate therefore that the same people should be drawn into a confrontation with the most unsympathetic railway official in England. To say that Churchman was unpopular before the strike took place is to barely hint at the truth. Born in the centre of rural James Herriott country, at West Rounton near Northallerton, he was pigeonholed by the NER management into this industrial landscape almost certainly because he was an outsider and therefore unlikely to have much truck with local discontent. From that perspective he was the perfect choice. He had no time for either coal miners or trade unions, particularly those union members who took part in industrial action. In consequence, he went out of his way to antagonise the striking men by encouraging and brazenly applauding the deployment of blackleg labour. Temperature reached boiling point on 20 August when he confronted a picket line outside the station concourse. Shaking a fist and hurling abuse at his erstwhile colleagues on the picket line, he made his position regarding the justice of the men's claim abundantly clear.[63] The men responded in kind. They pursued him to the end of the platform where he took refuge in a signal box with a stout lockable door. He should from then on have kept his head down. Instead, and bearing in mind there was a mob baying for his blood just beyond the walls, he stood by the window mocking the crowd, slowly and deliberately eating his substantial lunch with exaggerated enthusiasm. The object of this award-winning performance was to demonstrate that, unlike the starving men outside, he remained a wage-earner and could therefore afford to eat well. Suitably incensed by all this, the strikers attacked the signal box utilising anything they could lay their hands on, smashing the windows with ballast pulled from the track bed.[64] Unable to gain access to the building, the mob moved off into the nearby marshalling yard where they boarded a stationary coal train manned by blacklegs, making ready to depart. They threw the driver and fireman off the footplate and rendered the engine inoperable by dousing the fire. Churchman, meanwhile, had seen the coast was clear and legged it for home. He lived just a short distance away in Soho Cottages, now part of Locomotion and the same row of cottages in which the Hackworths had lived (Timothy and his brother Thomas Hackworth had lived in No. 1 Soho Cottages. Churchman occupied no.4.)

Shildon Station signal box – scene of the unfortunate sandwich incident.

Unfortunately, the mob spotted him and followed him home. They then laid siege to his house, subjecting it to a similar assault to that sustained by the signal box.

The end-product of all this was that 200 soldiers of the Enniskillen Fusiliers were despatched to Shildon with instructions to man and guard the station, signal boxes and marshalling yard. Even so, and despite their presence, strikers were able the following day to board a loaded coal train, awaiting departure from the yard, and eject the crew, just as they had the day before. They went further this time, releasing the brakes on a line of coal trucks at the top of the Brusselton incline, which careered downhill and collided with the wagons assembled in the yard; to the presumed consternation of the troops guarding them. A police bodyguard was assigned to Churchman to protect him from his former colleagues, who lined up on both sides of the railway track hurling stones and abuse at each train that went by. Stones were also thrown at Churchman from the platform opposite his office but he escaped unscathed.[65] One of the blackleg drivers was less fortunate. Hauled from the cab of his locomotive, his Company crest-emblazoned coat was torn off his back and cut up into little pieces, which were displayed like trophies on the chests of the men who defrocked him.

Press photographs show Enniskillen soldiers standing disconsolately on the station platform and peering morosely from

Enniskillen Fusiliers on duty at Shildon Station, during the 1911 national railway strike (picture courtesy of Beamish).

the parapets of railway bridges. They wouldn't be disconsolate or morose for long as the strike ended after just three days and the railwaymen, grievances unresolved, returned to work. As might be expected, their dispute over work conditions didn't end there. The same workers were out on strike the following year, although on this occasion industrial action was restricted just to employees of the NER. Anger bubbled on or just below the surface for a further three years, with hostilities postponed only for the duration of the Great War. Less than a year after it ended, in September 1919, NER employees were out on strike again with the employer once again drawing upon blackleg labour to fulfil key roles, a situation that would be repeated across the country in the general strike of 1926, with the men's anger now directed against the incoming regime of the London and North Eastern Railway (LNER).[66] As an employer, the LNER proved little better than the NER in terms of man-management. When the industrial slump of 1930 began to seriously affect its profits, the Company dismissed 375 Shildon men without consultation. A further 300 went in 1932, when for a few weeks wagon production at Shildon ceased altogether.[67] It took the onset of another war before a reluctant armistice was declared between management and employees. For the whole of the Second World War, the LNER came under the direct control of the government and strike action was declared illegal. This law continued to apply right through to 1951.[68] The outcome was an apparent period of industrial quiet with, on the surface, an 'all hands to the pump' attitude prevailing. What seems more likely is that industrial disquiet smouldered along underneath, however there was certainly no co-ordinated union action during this period. This may have reflected the warm relationship between the rail unions and the radical post-war Labour Government. So it wasn't until 1955, when the Conservatives were back in power, that the next major walk-out occurred, when the National Union of Railwaymen (NUR) called out all their members over an inter-union demarcation issue.

The years at Shildon when there was least industrial strife were, ironically, those anxious twilight years before the Works closed for good. The Wagon Works men were well aware that the future of the plant hung by a thread and prudently decided to take no precipitous action that might provoke retaliation from the hostile occupier of 10 Downing Street. A toothless 'Works Action Committee' was set up to promote the interests of the men during this difficult time, with the vain hope they would somehow be able to negotiate with their employer without confrontation, and hence lessen the impact of any decision made on the Works' future. Unsurprisingly, the Committee's efforts, whatever they amounted to, made scant difference to the outcome and the Works closed for good in 1984. In each year of its existence a quarter of the town's population had been employed in the Wagon Works and we may judge its significance to the town from the following moving account of young Ron Spedding's first day at work in 1940. He left home at 6.30 am:

'It was bitterly cold outside, the lowly streets lay under a white blanket of sparkling frost, illuminated by a full moon and clear sky full of twinkling stars. It seemed strange to me to see the moon and stars in the morning. But it was an experience I was to witness for the next 42 winters. The streets were so quiet that the very steady tread of my hobnailed boots muffled by the ground frost sounded unnatural. As I proceeded, men appeared out of the shadows to move in the same direction as myself; a door would open to reveal a shaft of light and a figure silhouetted for a moment, then the door would close and the figure move forward to join the general flow. As I approached the Works the number of figures increased rapidly until I was surrounded by a mass of humanity. The streets now reverberated to the sound of nearly 2,000 men. Four thousand hobnailed boots were beating out a rhythm on the cold morning air. To my mind, at that time, it sounded like an army on the move, which indeed it was; an army of working men all in similar dress bound for the same destination. As we entered the Works' gates the steam buzzer blew, with insistent clarity, giving all present a loud reminder that another working day had just begun.'

There can be no more eloquent evocation of a landscape irretrievably lost.

CHAPTER TEN

Innovation and experimentation

NER Tyneside
Electric No.1 at
Locomotion.

It could be said that, as far as the history of railways is concerned, Shildon has always been an experimenter and innovator, in the sense that no earlier railways were sufficiently advanced to prepare the railway company for what they were about to undertake. If Robert Stephenson's *Rocket* had pointed the way forward in terms of locomotive engineering, it was Hackworth's *Royal George* at New Shildon that most notably demonstrated the potential of steam as a transport medium. *Royal George* had several unique features. By coupling its six wheels, the power generated by its two cylinders was distributed throughout the length of the locomotive, thereby increasing wheel traction and reducing wasteful wheel slippage. Stephenson's early locos had been fitted with wooden spoked wheels, like the cartwheels upon which their design was based, and these constantly needed repair. Hackworth replaced them with his robust 'plug wheels', made by casting separate inner and outer metal sections then joining the two pieces with bolts and plugs to produce a sturdy composite. The crucial addition was a malleable wrought iron tyre shrunk around the rim. It is a tribute to the quality of the plug wheels that they became an essential feature of S&DR locos for many years, whether the locomotives in question were made at Shildon or elsewhere. The big leap forward, however, was Hackworth's blast pipe. This utilised the force created from ejecting exhausted steam through a constricted upturned tube placed directly in the flow of smoke in the chimney. The resulting increase in draught pulled more air through the fire, raising its temperature and generating additional steam. None of Hackworth's inventions either before or after, however, has generated more controversy than the blast pipe. Claims were made for blast pipe precedence for both Trevithick's locomotives and those of William Hedley, which Hackworth had worked on at Wylam. There is indeed some justification in the argument that the increased-draught phenomenon had been noted by Hedley and Trevithick although they took the matter no further. Therefore, it was left to Hackworth, who correctly interpreted the principle behind the effect, and made it fundamental to the way his engines worked. The blast pipe may have been the most important contribution Hackworth made to locomotive engineering, but it was hardly the last. To the above could be added his spring-operated pressure safety valve which replaced the crude weight-loaded seal used previously on engine boilers, including Stephenson's, that had proved so open to abuse whenever additional steam pressure was needed.

If New Shildon fathered the use and promotion of steam, therefore, it might come as a surprise to know it was also a pioneer in the use and promotion of electricity for powering its locomotive fleet. The 3 September 1915 issue of the *Yorkshire Post and Leeds Intelligencer* contained the following note, 'Experimental working on the electrified portion of the North-Eastern (*sic*) Railway from Shildon to Newport has commenced'.

On 1 July 1915 a major experiment in electric traction was about to begin. Steam haulage on a major North-East freight line was to give way to electricity. This wasn't the first electric railway experiment undertaken in Britain. The London Underground had been electrified, at least within its urban area, for many years, and even the NER could point to an isolated section of electrification, localised on Tyneside docks. What made the Shildon experiment so different, and special, was its scale. This project was intended from the outset to result in the nation's first electrified heavy-freight railway, and in consequence revolutionary locomotives would be needed. Given the timing, it might be thought this experimental railway was another product of the war effort. However, it had been planned long before war broke out. Nevertheless, it is fair to say that the sudden need for rapid transport of fuel from mine to coastal port focussed minds. So why was a move to electricity already on the cards? Well, electric locomotives offered distinct advantages over their steam counterparts; their rate of acceleration was greater, they required little preparation prior to start-up and most important of all they were simpler and easier to keep clean and maintain; a significant plus-point when manpower was suddenly in short supply.

The line chosen for electrification was the former Clarence Railway line, between Shildon and Stockton, which branched from the S&DR at Simpasture, a couple of miles east of Shildon. At the time, this section of the NER network was already dedicated to freight, and electrification could therefore be carried out with minimal inconvenience to the travelling public. It also offered the advantage of having no major gradients that novel, and untried, electrics would have to contend with. Ten new 74-ton electric locomotives, designed by Vincent Raven (shortly to be knighted), were built at the NER works at North Road, Darlington, and numbered 3-13 (the two smaller Tyneside electrics already having been allocated the numbers 1 and 2). Vincent Raven had been an early advocate of rail electrification. He was directly involved in the development of electrification of the NER on Tyneside and wanted to completely electrify the main line between York and Darlington; a feat he never achieved in his lifetime. In fact he died in 1934, just months before his Shildon to Newport experiment ended. In 1915, however, the future for wholesale electric traction looked promising.

In appearance, the new engines looked like heftier versions of their Newcastle cousins, one of which is currently on display at Locomotion, but the Shildon ten were far from mere dockside shunters. This new fleet was significantly more powerful, capable of hauling loads of up to 1,400 tons. They were built with a single central driver's cab with independent electric motors fore and aft mounted over two four-wheel bogies (the 'Bo-Bo' wheel arrangement). Electricity was supplied separately to each of the motors through pantographs connected to overhead cables. Work began in June 1913, with construction of the cable system, starting at Shildon engine shed roundhouse (No.3) and ending in the expansive Erimus marshalling yard complex next to the River Tees at Newport, Thornaby. The DC cables (1500 volts) were raised on poles 17½ feet above the rails, with the electricity generated by two privately owned sub-stations located near each end of the electrified section.

The first electrically driven train left Middridge sidings, Shildon, for Teesside on 1 July 1915 behind locomotive No.3 and, as predicted, in terms of efficiency in respect of cost/ton of coal shifted, the engines were a major success.[69] Indeed, it was Vincent Raven's claim that five Shildon electrics could accomplish the work of thirteen steam engines. On the strength of their subsequent performance, therefore, Raven designed and built an electric express passenger locomotive for use on what was anticipated to be a fully electrified trunk line between York and Darlington. Like the Shildon engines, the express engine prototype was built at Darlington's North Road Works and, just like its Shildon counterparts, it proved one experiment too far.

Shildon electric NER No.8 with Shildon engine sheds to the rear (picture courtesy of Science and Society Picture Library).

Intended for main line passenger traffic, 'No 13' (BR 26600 – yes it survived into BR days) it was a victim of the LNER's long term love affair with steam. It was tested on the Shildon-Newport electrified section but never used in anger. Its greatest claim to fame was that it took part in the 1925 S&DR centenary cavalcade, albeit suffering from the indignity of being hauled by a little 0-6-0 steam tank engine.

Nevertheless, in the first flush of youth the electrics were a revelation. Painted black to match their predicted cargo they worked four return trips from Shildon to Newport every day, being put to bed in one of the roundhouses at Shildon without the need for the elaborate end of day cleaning ritual and the mind-numbing start up procedures associated with their steam stablemates. Post-war pictures suggest that at least some of the class were repainted LNER apple green like the two Tyneside shunting engines, one of which is sporting that livery at Locomotion.

Since each loco was capable of hauling 1,400 tons of coal or more on each trip, this was viewed as a significant help to the war effort, even allowing that the engines were at first restricted to night-only working, to allow for daytime completion of the electrification programme. It looked like the future of the Shildon electrics was going to be bright and electrification of the main line between York and Darlington seemed the next logical step. Impressive in scope, the plan involved a combination of third rail and overhead electricity supply.[70] That the Shildon electrics were viewed as the way forward for railways is apparent from the fact that one of them (No.9) formed part of the locomotive cavalcade of 1925 to celebrate the centenary of the S&DR, although, since there was no overhead power supply on the cavalcade route, it had to be hauled by a Shildon steam loco, 0-6-0T J71 No.317.[71]

The demise of the experiment, when it came, was not due to any inadequacy in engine design or performance. As Harold Macmillan might have said, the decision to abandon the project was a consequence of 'events, dear boy, events'. Demand for coal had decreased steadily after the end of the war and the cost of maintaining an isolated electrified section located at the heart of a non-electric network increased accordingly, particularly after the company which provided the electricity, the Newcastle upon Tyne Electric Supply Company (NESCO), upped its charges significantly. On top of this there were the additional costs associated with day-to-day management and maintenance of the overhead cable system, all of which now needed either upgrade or replacement.

And finally, with less work around for the LNER's steam loco fleet, already capable of working the whole of the LNER network, the capital costs for replacing the engines and electrifying the entire system were just not worth the predicted returns. In consequence, despite the greater efficiency of the electric engines, they were now an expensive luxury; a luxury in the cash-strapped climate of the 1930s the Company could ill afford. There were also now other options which muddied the water. If they could eliminate the need for an overhead power supply but retain the virtues of the electric engines, they were on to a winner. As early as May 1929, therefore, the LNER began experimenting with diesel locomotives on Shildon to Middlesbrough freight trains. The results, almost predictably, looked encouraging; unfortunately a nationwide industrial recession followed by the outbreak of the Second World War meant it was many years before the diesel experiments bore fruit.[72]

Following the demise of the Shildon-Newport experiment the Shildon ten were mothballed at Darlington until, following the end of the war, they were rediscovered by the embryonic nationalised

BR electric 26020, last surviving stablemate of NER No.11, at the NRM at York.

British Railways, who considered modifying and relocating them somewhere in an already electrified section of the national rail network. Bearing this in mind, they were initially transferred from Darlington to Gosforth, on the electrified portion of the former LNER on Tyneside and given BR numbers 26502-11. There they sat for years awaiting their fate. If they had been sentient beings they would doubtless have been dismayed to find themselves unemployed while their diminutive cousins, the former NER electrics Nos. 1 and 2, strutted their stuff nearby. Eventually, in 1950, the decision was taken to scrap all the Shildon fleet apart from 26510 (originally No.11), which after modification, essentially replacing the two original independent pantographs with one, was transferred to Ilford in East London, where it re-entered service as a carriage shunting engine, a function it performed adequately until 1960. By then it was looking its age and would have needed an extensive and expensive rebuild to bring it up to scratch. Consequently, when money was lavished on the newer electrics in the yard, in 1963, to convert them from DC to AC, the decision was taken to scrap No.11. Given its history, it looked a prime candidate for preservation, being both a rail electric pioneer and the sole survivor of its type. However, this counted for nothing in the harsh economic climate of the sixties and it joined the growing queue of steam locos awaiting the scrapman's blow torch.

CHAPTER ELEVEN

Celebrations and commiserations

On the day (1 July 1925) the Duke and Duchess of York (the future King George VI and Queen Elizabeth) officially launched the S&DR centenary, the LNER issued an ultimatum to its staff. Unless they agreed to a 5 per cent reduction in their wages, there would be an 'unspecified' number of enforced redundancies.[73] For the men of Shildon this was not the only indignity they had to endure on the big day. Despite being the birthplace of the first conventional public railway anywhere in the world, Shildon was about to be ignored in the centenary celebrations. The sole acknowledgment of the Town's contribution had to wait until 5 December, when a plaque acknowledging Hackworth's contribution was unveiled at the Mason's Arms, in the presence of family members and railway dignitaries, including Timothy Hackworth's grandson and biographer, Robert Young. In July of that year, however, on a date that fitted better with the future king's personal plans than the correct centenary date of 27 September, a cavalcade of locomotives, ancient and modern, including a working replica of *Locomotion No. 1*,

BR 9F 2-10-0 *Evening Star* and 4MT 4-6-0 75029 outside Shildon Wagon Works, July 1975 (British Rail publicity picture).

was paraded before crowds on a straight stretch of line between Stockton and Darlington.

It was not the first time Shildon had been overlooked; the town was noticeably absent from the railway jubilee celebrations of 1875, when the nearest it got to feasting at the table was the presence of a couple of Shildon engines at a Darlington locomotive works open day at North Road, namely Hackworth's *Sanspareil* and the 1846 Bouch 0-6-0 *Shildon*. In fairness, Shildon's absence may also have had to do with the resurgence of smallpox in New Shildon, which, maintaining the railway connection, had recently taken the life of a girl working at the Mason's Arms. The presence of the disease had also been reported in a few houses nearby.

Well, at least the town's name was represented at Darlington and at least some of the Shildon workforce, provided they had a minimum of 10 years company service, were given the time off to attend, assuming they could afford to do so.

Shildon fared better in 1975.

Shildon Wagon Works, immediately prior to the 1975 locomotive cavalcade (picture courtesy of Brian Burns).

In August that year, 31 locomotives, including perhaps the most famous of them all, Gresley A3 *Flying Scotsman,* and the last steam locomotive built for the national network, 9F 2-10-0 *Evening Star,* sat steaming quietly in front of the shop doors of the Wagon Works. Temporarily the Wagon Repair Shop had become the engine shed

it once was. From 24-30 August it was laid open to the public, displaying the most impressive collection of steam locomotives assembled in one place in the last fifty years. For this particular railway celebration, Shildon was finally at the heart of proceedings. Thousands gathered near the Works and alongside the track from New Shildon to Heighington, to applaud Shildon's outstanding contribution to railways. On the days preceding the cavalcade, a couple of locomotives even gave the visiting public rides between the marshalling yards and the works. 34 engines turned out in total on the day, and representing the original pioneers was a working replica of *Locomotion*, albeit with additional safety features the original could only have dreamed of, such as brakes. The parade began at 2pm on the 31st. The 33 steam locomotives and solitary diesel which formed the cavalcade, in the order in which they appeared, is as follows, the numbers quoted being those they carried during the parade (It should be noted, however, that some of these engines have since been given their final British Railways numbers e.g. K1 '2005' is now '62005'.)

1) Stephenson 0-4-0, *Locomotion* (or at least its working replica)
2) NCB J94 0-6-0 No.2502
3) Stanier Black 5 4-6-0 No.4767
4) Raven Q6 0-8-0 No.2238
5) Worsdell J27 0-6-0 No.2392
6) Gresley K1 2-6-0 No.2005
7) Caledonian 0-4-4T No.419
8) Gresley D49 4-4-0 No.246, *Morayshire*
9) 5700 class 0-6-0PT No.7752
10) Manor class 4-6-0 No.7808, *Cookham Manor*
11) Modified Hall Class 4-6-0 No.6960, *Raveningham Hall*
12) Gresley V2 No.4771, *Green Arrow*
13) Thompson B1 4-6-0 No.1306
14) Stanier 8F 2-8-0 No.8233
15) Ex-WD Austerity 2-10-0 No.600
16) Gresley A4 4-6-2 No. 4498, *Sir Nigel Gresley*
17) Stirling 4-2-2 No.1
18) Gresley A3 4-6-2 No.4472, *Flying Scotsman*
19) Fletcher 2-4-0 No. 910
20) Atlantic 4-4-2 No. 990
21) Precedent class 2-4-0 No.790, *Hardwicke*
22) Midland Compound 4-4-0 No.1000

23) Stanier 4-6-2 No.6201, *Princess Elizabeth*
24) Jubilee 4-6-0 No.5690, *Leander*
25) Wantage Tramway 0-4-0 No.5
26) Aspinall 0-4-0ST No.51218
27) Stroudley A1X 0-6-0ST, *Fenchurch*
28) Merchant Navy class 4-6-2 No.35028, *Clan Line*
29) Urie S15 class 4-6-0 No.841
30) Ivatt 4MT class 2-6-0 No.43106
31) Stanier 2-6-2ST No. 41241
32) BR Standard 4MT 4-6-0 No.75029
33) BR 9F class 2-10-0 No.92220, *Evening Star*
34) Experimental HST train[74]

To claim the event was well supported would be a gross underestimation. According to the *Daily Express*, 300,000 people visited Shildon on Cavalcade Day, as opposed to Shildon's normal resident population of 15,000.[75] According to the correspondent:

'British Railways had laid on 17 special trains and the car queues outside the town stretched into the distance. Visitors from several countries were logged in the official statistics -including two jumbo jet loads arriving on charter from Japan.'

The canny local entrepreneurs were also out in force. Quoting from the same source:

'You couldn't get through Shildon without buying something – railway tea towels, locomotive picture postcards, books, key fobs, ash trays, car badges, cuff links, ties or simply an empty tin with a locomotive label.'

The watching public were in raptures. As one female spectator put it:

'Trains… I could look at them forever. I love just everything about them – the colours, the smell. And they put people in such a happy mood don't they?'

Apart from the use of the word 'trains' when she meant 'locomotives', amen to that.

Less prescient was the report in the *Northern Echo* which stated:

'At Shildon, County Durham, from 24 until 31 August will be seen the largest collection of steam locomotives assembled in this country for fifty years. *It could well be the last as the electrification programme of British Rail may prohibit the movement of these large locomotives in the future.*'(my italics)

In 1975, who would have predicted either the growth in number and popularity of heritage railways or the public's enthusiasm for steam 'specials' on the national rail network.

If the future for the survival of steam locomotives in 1975 was uncertain, the future for Shildon looked good. Whilst the Beeching axe was falling on the rail network in the North-East, the line from Darlington to Bishop Auckland, despite being originally scheduled for closure, somehow survived along with the Wagon Works. Expensive new equipment was even introduced in the 1960s, including four new metal cutting machines in 1968 which doubled the output from the works, ensuring that the machinery at the Works remained state-of-the art. This was reflected in orders for rolling stock which reached record proportions, with overall

***Sanspareil* replica,** built by Shildon Works apprentices for the 1979 re-enactment of the Rainhill Trials (picture courtesy Jane Hackworth-Young).

productivity increasing by 300 per cent. When the engineering arm of the railway system, British Rail Engineering Ltd. (BREL), was created in 1970, the future of the works looked secure. Apart from the existing lucrative contracts with nationalised industries including the Central Electricity Generating Board (CEGB), the Works now embraced a global market which had recently included 150 high tech wagons for Malaya and by the standards of the time the Company was a significant UK foreign currency earner. 1979 was the 150th anniversary of the Rainhill Trials and the Company felt sufficiently chipper to permit their young apprentices to take time off to build a replica *of Sanspareil* to take part in the re-enactment of the Trials at Liverpool.

Unfortunately, nationalised industries didn't figure in the plans of the Thatcher Government. On paper, the Works seemed to tick all the right boxes for survival. It had an established market in the UK and an expanding market overseas and a technically able workforce on the doorstep. What's not to like? Its Achilles' heel, however, was BREL. The economics of BREL was less clear cut. Much of its business was not profitable and, being an industry owned by the nation, it was in the firing line following the election of a Conservative Government with a zeal for privatisation. There was little indication on the surface that the axe was about to fall when the Works held an open day to celebrate 150 years of its existence (albeit that this was in reality the 158th year since the works creation). The BREL management even paid a glowing tribute to the works' and its loyal workforce:

> 'The staff of Shildon Wagon Works ask you to join them today in commemorating 150 years service to Railways and pay tribute to all those railwaymen and women who throughout the years have been loyal servants of the Shildon Works.'

To no avail. Within two weeks of being awarded a multimillion pound contract to supply wagons to the Congo and barely nine months after the BREL works open day, on 29 June 1984, Shildon Wagon Works officially closed. Completion of outstanding orders meant that the business carried on for a couple more months before the men were finally laid off. Before the end came a Works deputation was dispatched to 10 Downing Street to argue against the comical financial arguments being used for closure. Petitions containing thousands of signatures in support of the Works were handed in. The local Labour MP, Derek Foster, even tried to organise a management buy-out, involving local business men and trade union officials, but it was too little, too late. In the cut and thrust world of Thatcher economics, Shildon's face just didn't fit and more than 2,000 people in an area of high unemployment lost their livelihood.

Despite the doom and gloom, Shildon continues to stage memorable events for the rail enthusiast. In February 2014, there was the 'Great Goodbye' (or 'Final Farewell' depending upon which promotional brochure you read) when all the surviving Gresley A4s assembled for inspection at Locomotion, and in July 2016 Locomotion staged a 'shed bash' for trainspotters. Shed bashes, for the uninitiated, were events in the 1950s and 60s where groups of trainspotters would travel great distances to descend on engine sheds in force (sometimes illegally) and collect the numbers of as many steam locos as possible before they vanished forever – the locos that is, not the trainspotters.

The 'Great Goodbye' at Locomotion. North American visitors, the Gresley A4s *Dominion of Canada* and *Dwight D. Eisenhower*, enjoy a brief holiday in their native land before heading home.

The idea was to recreate the period feel of the 1960s with engines in steam in British Railways livery. The centrepiece was the Gresley A3, *Flying Scotsman*, resplendent in BR green and bearing its British Railways number '60103' as in the last days of steam on the national network, fondly remembered by old trainspotters such as myself. Equally notable was the presence of the streamlined A4, *Union of South Africa*, the two engines being double headed for public trips along the length of track between Locomotion and the historic western end of the site. Representing freight engines from the North-East, and also in steam on the day, were Q6 0-8-0 63395 and J72 0-6-0T 69023. The facilities provided at Shildon for visiting steam engines, i.e. immediate access to the national rail network and a resident support team of trained and knowledgeable railway volunteers ensure that 'steam days' will be a regular feature for the foreseeable future if the powers that be allow it to be so.

It was intimated as recently as 2014 that one site of the Science Museum Group which manages five museums, including the Science Museum at South Kensington, might lose funding because of government cuts. Staff and voluntary groups at Locomotion were particularly concerned because of Locomotion's location in a non-tourist area, and the fact it was an offshoot of the NRM at York would suggest it would not attract the necessary public interest to ensure its survival. What has saved Locomotion in the end is sheer visitor numbers. In its first year alone, Locomotion attracted 250,000 visitors and, in the years following, the numbers have held up well. It seems that the national need for nostalgia has never been greater and Shildon, as the world's first railway town, has seized the initiative.

CHAPTER TWELVE

Shildon as a railway heritage centre

In 1923, two years before the S&DR centenary celebrations, the idea of a 'national' railway museum was already being considered. Since railways as we know them began in the North-East, the only question was where in the extensive network of the LNER it could best be accommodated.[76] Darlington seemed the obvious choice, in terms of both history and accessibility, but the town was rejected in favour of London or York where the seats of power within the Company lay. Museums had housed railway memorabilia before of course, not least the Science Museum in South Kensington where *Puffing Billy* amongst others was resident, but eventually York was selected, and railway enthusiasts of my own generation have fond memories of visiting the Railway Museum housed in a former carriage shed, in Queen Street, just south of York station. This became the nearest thing to a dedicated railway museum in the country following the creation of British Railways.

Over the years, York established itself as the home of railway heritage with parties of visitors travelling there from all over the world, its growth only limited by the availability of suitable space in which to house large exhibits. Following the end of steam in the sixties, the old loco roundhouse in Leeman Road sat vacant, awaiting the decision as to its fate. Once the government agreed to fund a National Railway Museum, it required little thought to choose the redundant roundhouse as its location, despite bids from other railway centres including London. The National Railway Museum at York soon proved to be a victim of its own success. It was inundated with railway memorabilia, including large exhibits such as iconic steam locomotives, far more indeed than it could possibly display in the space available. So, the search for an additional museum site began.

Nobody knows who first suggested the idea of a railway museum at Shildon but it is certain the 150th anniversary of the opening of the S&DR focussed minds. Unlike the centenary event of 1925, Shildon was now the centre of activities. It was unfortunate, therefore,

Two sad views of New Shildon in the early 1970s. 1) Looking west towards Shildon railway station with the former line to Shildon Wagon Works, now with rails removed, to the left and 2) the semi-derelict Soho Cottages (Pictures courtesy of Jane Hackworth-Young).

that Shildon's formidable railway heritage was under serious threat. Planning permission had recently been granted for a new road into the heart of the town which, if implemented, necessitated the demolition of the entire row of terraced railway houses which included the former home of the Hackworth family and William Bouch,

Soho Cottage. Recently vacated, these council owned properties had slipped into dereliction and were boarded up, awaiting demolition. In fact, it was only because of funding problems with the road project that they were still standing. This was the situation that pertained when two descendants of Timothy Hackworth, his great-grandson Reginald Hackworth Young and Reginald's daughter Jane, visited Shildon. They were there to trace their Hackworth roots whilst paying respects at Timothy's grave. By the time they arrived at Shildon, in the summer of 1972, the application for the road scheme had lapsed but the project was still very much on the cards. The family met the vicar of All Saints Church in Old Shildon and were shown Hackworth's grave, which was now as dilapidated as Soho Cottages, which they also visited. This seemed surprising as the Hackworth name then, as today, was still venerated in the town. There was a statue of the great man in the local recreation ground, and in July 1950, there was even an open air service of commemoration to mark the centenary of his death, including the laying of a wreath on his grave by the recently crowned 'Britain's Railway Queen', Miss J.E. Hubbard, followed by a Hackworth-themed open day at the wagon works on the following Sunday.[77]

Following the Hackworth family visit to Shildon a meeting was quickly arranged with Walter Nunn, Chairman of Shildon Town Council, to try and safeguard Soho Cottage and set up some sort of permanent memorial to Timothy. Nunn was sympathetic to the idea of preserving Soho Cottage as part of a heritage museum, particularly in view of the forthcoming railway celebrations, so it was a good thing that the cottage was currently in the ownership of the council, which made discussions about its future tenable. Sadly, much of Shildon's railway heritage had already been lost. Nothing remained, for example, of Hackworth's original Soho Works, although there were still a handful of buildings standing in the vicinity which dated from those far off days. These included a former NER goods depot and the structure known as the 'engine shed', which was the building once used as a gym by the Railway Institute and previously an engine paint shop. Soho Shed as it is now called was particularly intriguing in that it dated from a time before Soho Works. It was built in 1826 for metal storage by Kilburn's Iron Foundry, at some point may have been leased by Timothy Hackworth for Soho Works, and was eventually purchased by the S&DR in 1855. These few buildings, the last examples of New Shildon's railway origins, were about to disappear unless something could be done quickly. A campaign to save them began, fronted by Reginald Hackworth Young who contacted anyone who he thought might be interested in conserving the site, including Sedgefield Council, Durham County Council and the local MP. Also supporting the campaign was Arthur Stabler whose family had worked on the Railway since the day *Locomotion* first set forth from the Mason's Arms crossing. Indeed, one of Arthur's ancestors was the fireman on Stephenson's engine that day and another of his forebears accompanied John Wesley Hackworth on his perilous Russian expedition. Also backing the proposal, fortuitously, was Walter Nunn who was appointed Vice Chairman of the Sedgefield Urban Council committee, and would oversee the 150th anniversary arrangements.

To save Soho Cottage there had to be sound reasons against its demolition. The building had been neglected and largely forgotten to the extent that even most local people didn't recognise its historical significance. There was one obvious solution. If there

Queen Elizabeth the Queen Mother opens the Timothy Hackworth Museum, 17 July 1975 (Picture courtesy Jane Hackworth-Young).

was to be some permanent memorial to Timothy Hackworth in the town then where better than his former home. Major restoration work, both internal and external, would be needed to restore what had been until recently an old damp council house to its original state. There was also the question of finance. Although the timing of the project, given the pending S&DR anniversary, meant that at least some local authority contribution was possible, in the end much of the refurbishment cost had to be borne by the English Tourist Board. Finally, there was a decision to be made as to how the interior would be restored. Unsurprisingly, Hackworth's descendants wanted the rooms to be reconstructed as they would have looked during Hackworth's time. In support of this, there were boxes of Hackworth memorabilia which could be immediately displayed, and Bowes Museum had offered the loan of period furniture, including a grandfather clock. By the time of the official opening, four fully furnished rooms were ready to show to Her Majesty the Queen Mother, who officially declared the Timothy Hackworth Museum open on 17 July 1975, two months before the opening of the National Railway Museum at York. Agreement had coincidentally been reached on saving the other two surviving buildings from Hackworth's time, with the idea of extending the museum complex. There was even a surviving Hackworth engine in Shildon which could be put on display, the mysterious *Braddyll,* which, according to a repair plate found on the engine by Michael Bailey and John Glithero, who made a detailed study of the locomotive remains, at some time was also called *Nelson. Braddyll,* the name by which it was known at the National Coal Board (NCB), took its moniker from one of the proprietors of South Hetton Colliery. There is no record of either a *Nelson* or *Braddyll* ever having been purchased by that company. However, there was a Hackworth designed and built 0-6-0 called *Buddle* known to have been sold to the colliery in 1840 and the two engines may eventually prove to be one and the same.

More has been written and argued over about *Braddyll* than is capable of sensible discussion here. The known facts are that the carcase of an old locomotive was inherited from the NCB. It had worked at South Hetton Colliery until 1875 after which time it was converted into a snow plough. For much of the first half of the twentieth century it lay abandoned, although its antiquity was noted, and it was scheduled for preservation in 1948 by an official of the Coal Board.[78] *Braddyll* is a strange beast. It is, transparently, the shell of a typical Hackworth

0-6-0 freight locomotive fitted with his archetypal 'plug' wheels. Almost everything else about the engine is up for grabs. It has even been suggested that the boiler was turned through 180° to present a squarer face to snow drifts to assist ploughing. Even its original manufacturer has been called into question, with suggestions it may have been built by George Fossick and Thomas Hackworth at Stockton and not at Timothy's factory at Shildon. For years it stood on a plinth next to the entrance to the Lambton Engine Works at Philadelphia before being moved to a site opposite the Shildon Town Council offices in Burke Street. It has finally (hopefully) found a permanent home in Soho Shed at the Soho Cottage end of Locomotion.

If the world's attention was on Shildon in 1975, interest faded somewhat after the S&DR 150th anniversary celebrations ended, yet despite this, a steady stream of visitors to the Timothy Hackworth Museum over the following decade showed that the idea of a functioning museum, albeit off the normal tourist track, was sound. A 1925 biography of Hackworth, written by grandson Robert Young, was updated by Hackworth's direct descendants, Jane Hackworth- Young and Ulick Loring, and reissued by

Hackworth 0-6-0
Braddyll at South Hetton Colliery (NCB picture).

the recently formed Hackworth Society where it sold well. Meanwhile down at York, the National Railway Museum, despite two extensions, had expanded to the point there was insufficient room to display all the large exhibits they had in storage. Under pressure from the government to make all their memorabilia accessible to the public, there was an added incentive to find additional space. Since there was nowhere suitable nearby, it was decided to search for another site. The spotlight turned on Shildon. Shildon was ideal for lots of reasons; it was after all where modern railways began and there was already a railway heritage museum there. It also had good rail connections as Shildon station was just a few minutes by train from the east coast main line at Darlington Bank Top. Finally, it had a proven capacity for attracting tourists and, crucially, had enough space for the construction of a large hall on spare land which had once been part of the marshalling yard. The hall, known as the Collections Building, together with the buildings west of the site including Soho House, Kilburn's Warehouse, the Coal Manager's Building, the Parcel Office, the Coal Drops and Black Boy Buildings became the museum 'Locomotion'. The project was a partnership between the NRM and Durham County Council, although no-one at the time seemed aware which partner was responsible for what. Locomotion was opened by Prime Minister Tony Blair in 2004 and since that day visitor numbers have far exceeded expectations. The highpoint was in February 2014, when 120,000 visitors came to the museum to drool over the six surviving streamlined Gresley A4s, which included *Mallard*, the fastest steam locomotive in the world. Two had been shipped across the Atlantic specially for the occasion, B.R. No.60008 *Dwight D. Eisenhower* and B.R. No.60010 *Dominion of Canada*. Both needed a little TLC before they could be presented to the public, particularly *Canada*, which was given a complete repaint job in Locomotion's workshop. The workshop there has been a revelation, teaching much needed engineering skills to local volunteers including at least one young apprentice.

Whilst Locomotion developed positively under the NRM umbrella, the former Timothy Hackworth Museum fared less well. In a mistaken attempt to modernise the museum's image, the interior of Soho Cottage was gutted, and the period furnishings replaced by static displays about Shildon's past, including a

The six surviving Gresley A4s line up outside Locomotion in July 2016 (picture courtesy Ken Hodgson).

constantly running video about the closure of the Wagon Works. If the sentiment behind the changes was laudable, the result was laughable and hardly merited the walk from the Collections Building where the main car park is located. The situation worsened; in its most recent incarnation Soho Cottage became just a collection of bare rooms and display boards, and now even this is closed to the public. Happily, it looks like matters are about to improve. The joint owners, the Science Museum (SMG), have come to an agreement with their partners, Durham County Council, on the way forward. The Bouch coal drops, which are crumbling, are being made safe and in return for providing 50 per cent of the funding needed for the long backlog of repairs to the historic buildings and structures, SMG will be granted a lease of 112 years. A conservation plan has also now been received from the project consultants, Alan Baxter.

All the boxes of Hackworth family correspondence, including irreplaceable communications between Timothy and George Stephenson, had been gathering dust in the upstairs rooms at Soho Cottage for many years, until the contents were eventually sorted and catalogued by Jane Hackworth-Young. They are now safely tucked away in the NRM's railway research facility at York, 'Search Engine'.

The other two surviving buildings have been dealt with more sympathetically, at least in the sense that their interiors have been restored to something approaching their original appearance.

The former NER goods depot at Locomotion.

Nonetheless, they attract fewer visitors than they ought to because the doors are locked most of the time, possibly because of lack of suitable volunteers to man the buildings. As mentioned earlier, *Braddyll*, with its own recent repaint job, is housed in Soho Shed, where, nearby, the former NER goods shed has become the western terminus for steam train rides on those occasions when projected visitor numbers warrant something more than static displays. At the eastern end of the site is the large hall known as the Collections Building where static exhibits including iconic locomotives such as the former LNER 2-6-2 *Green Arrow* and Southern Railway 4-6-2 *Winston Churchill* are housed.

Until recently a former Victorian Methodist Sunday school a few yards away also formed part of Locomotion. As the Museum's reception building, 'Welcome', it housed Hackworth's *Sanspareil*, previously displayed firstly at the Science Museum at South Kensington and later at the NRM at York. Amusingly, no-one had compared the size of *Sanspareil* with the size of the doors to the building until the day the engine was delivered. Finding no way of getting the loco inside, it had to be reloaded and taken back to storage until the Science Museum could work out a solution. Eventually part of the wall was removed to get *Sanspareil* safely tucked up inside. This would doubtless have been fine if the building was to be the engine's final resting place but unfortunately the procedure needed to be repeated, after *Sanspareil* was transferred yet again to the Collections building, where it now (2018) stands next to the statue of its creator, and on the opposite side of the aisle from its replica, the *Sanspareil* lookalike built by Wagon Works apprentices, which is 80 per cent the size of the original.

If you are ever lucky enough to visit Locomotion on a 'steam' day you can view the former coal drops close to. This impressive stone structure has undergone intermittent restoration over the years. Intermittent because of the availability of funding. The drops were even bigger in their day but the eastern end collapsed and was never restored. Close to the drops is a platelayers' hut and bank riders' cabin which also date from S&DR days and just beyond, at the end of the Shildon Station platform, is the signal box where

0-6-0T J72 BR 69023 passes the Bouch designed coal drops at Locomotion (picture courtesy Jane Hackworth-Young).

a belligerent Christopher Churchman defied his fellow railway workers in 1911. The land where the Gas Works and Soho Works once stood is now landscaped grassy banks beneath which lie the remains of the former Works. As to Locomotion, the Collections Building is impressive and here you can often see volunteers attempting some new railway-related restoration in the workshop at the eastern end. The 'Friends of the NRM' clean the rolling stock every week and often invite the public into the cabs of the locos to explain their operation. In the yard outside, amidst a mix of rolling stock and engines, there is always a selection of wagons that were built at Shildon, reflecting a time when the Town demonstrated what railways could achieve to the rest of the world.

When it comes to the fine detail of loco identification I freely admit I am found wanting. I can tell the difference between a streamlined Gresley A4, say, and a freight 0-6-0 such as a Q6 but there my trainspotting skills end. So, when I heard there was an ongoing project to build a G5 tank engine in Shildon from scratch I had to refer to my friendly Ian Allan books to find out what was on offer. For those, like me, not in the know, a few words about the G5. The G5s were 0-4-4 tank engines, built mostly at Darlington in the closing years of the reign of Queen Victoria, to the design of the North Eastern Railway's talented engineer Wilson Worsdell. Initially intended as shunting engines, they could often be seen pulling local passenger trains, including those that worked the branch line through Shildon from West Auckland to Darlington. Their heyday was in the years before the Second World War when there was hardly an engine shed in the North-East that didn't have a compliment of G5s, including the shed at Shildon. Prior to the arrival of the ubiquitous diesel multiple unit (DMU), G5s were a common sight at rural stations usually fronting a couple of elderly passenger coaches. This class had a long life; although more than half a century old at the time of nationalisation, nearly 150 survived into British Railways ownership, including one that had been at Shildon when the shed closed in 1935. This engine had been allocated the NER number 1737 but was renumbered 67273 by BR and survived until May 1957. When the last G5 was cut up at the scrapyard it seemed the G5s had gone forever, but it seems they had a friend in rail enthusiast Dr Mike Woods. Through his initiative there was a chance the world would get to see one more.

'Newbuild' steam locomotive projects are gaining popularity following the success of *Tornado*, the beautiful A1 express passenger

Richard Maughan, Brian Cox and Norman Raine, of the G5 project team, line up in front of the smokebox of newbuild G5 1759.

engine recently built at Darlington. *Tornado* represented a class of engines, like the G5, rendered extinct following the dieselisation and electrification of the national railway fleet. The idea of building a steam locomotive from first principles seemed improbable, not least because the technology no longer existed. In consequence, there were many that believed that *Tornado* would never be built, since no parts of the original A1s had survived. Every major component would have to be newly forged and the cost therefore was going to be astronomical. The *Tornado* project depended on the enthusiasm of volunteers with engineering skills, and financial support from steam locomotive buffs who wanted to see an A1 working again. The project, despite the projected cost, had a lot going for it. A handsome new express passenger steam engine would certainly be in demand, and heritage railway work meant money. Would this also be true for a newbuild G5? Time will only tell, but the Friends of the G5 certainly believe so. Like *Tornado*, every component part would have to be made from scratch referring to old engineering drawings, since nothing had survived from the original locomotives. First, the project team needed a location where a new engine could be built. Inevitably with an end-product of this size they needed somewhere with decent access for large vehicles and lots of assembly space. By a nice serendipity, at least in the context of this book, this was going to be Shildon. The G5, described on the Friends' promotional leaflet as 'the lost legend of the N.E railways', was coming home.

Scattered across the Hackworth Industrial Estate at Shildon are fragments of the Shildon Wagon Works, around which the estate developed. Opposite the remnants of what was once the Lift and Brake Shop, one of the new factory units has been dedicated to bringing the G5 back to life. There, in September 2017, I met promoters of the project, Richard Maughan (CEO), Norman Raine and Brian Cox. Of these, Richard is the only one with prior hands-on engineering experience in building steam locomotives. This he gained at Philadelphia, a steam heritage centre in Tyne and Wear not too far away from the current site. He also recently worked on model engines at the now defunct Great Northern Steam project and was keen to get involved in something life size. Virtually the whole of the shop floor in the assembly unit at Shildon is taken up with locomotive parts, like some giant Meccano set. Here a boiler, there a set of wheels, over there the engine's cab. Centrepiece is the frame and fitted smokebox, so on the first Saturday of the month the visiting public can immediately see that a steam loco is under construction. Assembled is the correct word here, because all the parts are manufactured elsewhere. The distinctive G5 smokebox, for example, was built at I.D. Hewitt of Wakefield. Nearby is the new boiler, invariably the most expensive component, waiting to be fitted to the frame. In fact, the only outstanding expensive components still to be sourced are the cylinders and linkage. Given a fair wind and the money needed to purchase the remaining pieces, therefore a new G5 could be moving under its own steam within 18 months. At the time of going to press the engine is to be painted in NER livery and carry the next sequential identification number to its long-lost sisters, number

'1759'. I asked what the owners are planning to do with the engine once built. As I might have expected they intend to lease it out to heritage railways and 'working' museums. Since Locomotion fits nicely into that category, perhaps in a couple of years we might just see a G5 at work in Shildon again, turning the clock back eighty years. The icing on the cake for me would be if the engine, even if only occasionally, carried the number '1737'. Then it would really have come home.

On the same day I met the G5 team, I dropped in on the workshop at Locomotion. Four men were working on the restoration of a London urban commuter coach dating from the late '50s. It had originally been part of a two-coach electric unit, the frumpy sister of which was parked out in front of the museum looking derelict and forlorn. The revamp of these two units is part of a project designed to illustrate the contribution made to society by urban trains, particularly in London; the trains which daily transport hundreds of thousands to their workplace. So why is Shildon involved?

Class 414 urban electric unit awaits restoration in the workshop at Locomotion.

The Science Museum has long been associated with the preservation and restoration of historic machines. Stephenson's *Rocket*, Hedley and Hackworth's *Puffing Billy* and Hackworth's *Sanspareil* were all renovated and put on display by technicians at South Kensington; in appearance at least looking like they were during their working life. After the LNER railway museum at York was absorbed into the Science Museum Group, the resident large exhibits were transferred to York's former roundhouse. It was a natural consequence, therefore, that the restoration formerly conducted on old locomotives should move with them. A new workshop was built next to the roundhouse where visitors could observe, from a viewing gallery, the restoration work in progress. This included the major project of reconstructing *Flying Scotsman* to the point where it could be put back in steam. To this day York remains *Scotsman*'s home, a place to which it returns whenever repairs or a facelift are required. It seems today that the public's reaction to this costly and controversial project has more than justified the outlay. *Flying Scotsman* is still *the* major showpiece for heritage railways, regularly working on such railways or appearing in news items and documentary films about the heyday of steam. The project was considered 'controversial' because it was felt that at a time when public money for museums was scarce, the million plus outlay for *Flying Scotsman*'s restoration could be better spent elsewhere.

There was obvious public support for the sort of facilities and expertise provided by the NRM's workshop at York but with only limited capacity for such engineering work, eyes turned to Shildon and the new Collections Building.

One corner of Locomotion was therefore set aside as a workshop where ongoing projects could be viewed by visitors from an adjacent ramped walkway. It was at the workshop I met Richard Pearson, who leads a team of 18 recruited locally for restoration work. Nearly all his team are unpaid volunteers, with just two full time Science Group employees, Richard, and Shildon resident Jeff Cail along with occasional government funded apprentices. Virtually none of the volunteers were originally qualified in the specialist skills needed for restoring railway vehicles, but with the support of short-term, project-specific, engineers they more than manage to get by. I asked what the work involved, given the lack of directly relevant expertise amongst the recruits, and was told that most restoration work is in fact unskilled, involving just the removal of rust and the scraping away of peeling paint. This is less boring than it might sound when, for

Jeff Cail and Richard Pearson, of the Locomotion workshop team, in front of the Class 414 urban electric unit under restoration.

example, the clean-up job you're involved in is the aforementioned restoration of the Gresley A4, *Dominion of Canada*.

Dominion of Canada, in particular, required a complete makeover which involved not only the removal of all loose paint and rust but the restoration of the overall appearance of the engine to its pre-war LNER state, with its striking blue livery and additional streamlining in the form of purpose-built valances over the driving wheels. The loco had taken a bit of a battering over the years and required 30 gallons of plastic filler to regain its original shape. After replacing the more recent double chimney with the single chimney it had in LNER days, the crowning feature was the addition of the warning bell in front of the smokebox, which it was obliged to carry when working in Canada and America. Lined up beside its sister A4s in front of the large exhibit building at the time of the 'Great Goodbye', *Canada* was a fitting tribute to the skill and enthusiasm still evident in the DNA of Shildon railwaymen.

Most of the projects undertaken at Locomotion are less iconic but no less important. The same team recently completed the restoration

of the coach used by Winston Churchill during the Second World War. It is currently (as of 2018) on display near to the Southern Railway Battle of Britain 4-6-2, named after the great man, which pulled his funeral train. Coach restoration is a major part of the volunteers' remit, hence the current project, carried out on behalf, and jointly funded by, the Science Museum and Network South East Railway Society. The two Class 414 electric train units had been stored outside following withdrawal from service twenty years ago and were in a sorry state when they arrived at Shildon. On the day I visited the workshop, restoration work was in progress on the leading coach. The original fittings had been removed and many of the metal floor panels were being replaced because of corrosion. It looked, to me, that there was a lot of work needed to restore the vehicle to anything resembling its original state. Since the two coaches are to form a static exhibit at York, one side will be painted at Shildon in the original British Railways blue and grey livery and the other in Network Rail's colours of blue and white, which seemed a bit odd to my mind but there you are. The men of the workshop

Winston Churchill's coach, restored to pristine condition at Locomotion.

are never short of projects. It is fitting that one of the 'carousel' coal wagons built for the NCB at Shildon was restored to its original state by the Locomotion workshop people. It was purchased by the 'Friends of the NRM' (NE Branch) and brought to Shildon from Wales. It is on display nearby. In the yard outside, the last wagon to emerge from Shildon Wagon Works awaits its turn for a facelift. At coffee break in the workshop, I chatted with the men as they came and went. They all seemed to be enjoying themselves despite the hard and dirty work they undertook. The end-product of their labours was all around. More power to their elbow.

Epilogue

In April 2016 I joined a small walking group, led by Caroline Hardie and Jane Hackworth-Young representing the Friends of The Stockton and Darlington Railway (FoSDR), who were trialling a series of walks along the first 26 miles of the old railway. We met outside the Collections Building at Locomotion and followed the footpath alongside the Network Rail line past the current railway station and Soho Cottage. There are promising plans in the pipeline for the Cottage. At the time of writing it is just a shell, and visitors gain little insight into how it looked inside at the time Timothy was living there. The idea is to restore the interior and make it a better attraction for visitors to Shildon. A path from the former Soho Works site follows the line of the old Black Boy Branch

Recreating the past: J21 0-6-0 65033, representative of a class of freight engines which were once a common sight at Shildon, in the former marshalling yard, now part of Locomotion.

north alongside the deep cutting that carries the Darlington line on to Bishop Auckland via Shildon Tunnel. Near the top of the hill, where the incline's engine house used to be, there is a solitary S&DR coal chaldron on a plinth and, nearby, a few one storey cottages which once housed railway staff. Further along the road into Old Shildon is the building which had been Dan Adamson's coach house, the man who operated the horse drawn passenger service used in the first years of the S&DR, and a little further on is the churchyard where Timothy Hackworth, his wife, second son Timothy and his work colleague John Graham are buried, no doubt conversing for eternity on railway matters. For those interested in railways, Shildon still has lots to offer.

It has become fashionable recently to downplay the contribution made by the S&DR in the development of railways. For some, the events of 27 September 1825 were just another step along the rocky road to today's railways; the principal contender for the title 'First Modern Railway' being the Liverpool and Manchester Railway (L&MR). This is, of course, errant nonsense. It was largely because of the success of the S&DR with dynamic input from George Stephenson that steam haulage finally won out on the L&MR. Even as late as 1829 the Directors of the L&MR were considering the possible use of a sequence of rope linked stationary engines to move their rolling stock, in a similar way to the system employed at Brusselton and Etherley inclines.

There were steam hauled railways long before the S&DR, and there were bigger and better railways long after, including it must be conceded the L&MR, whose vision and scope surpassed anything that occurred on that fateful day at Shildon. This is neither here nor there. The crucial difference is that all the principles of today's railways were established on *Locomotion's* first historic journey from New Shildon to Stockton. What came before was experimentation and what came after merely refinements and improvements, however impressive these might have been. The opening of the S&DR was the watershed. After September 1825, there was no going back. This was recognised at the time and has been acknowledged in all subsequent national railway anniversaries, including the one proposed for 2025.

Interest in Shildon's railway heritage grows year on year, even if what remains is under constant threat from both local neglect and the interest of property developers. Fighting to save its railway legacy are the volunteers who labour under the banner of the Friends of the Stockton and Darlington Railway (FoSDR). Events, such as organised walks, are regularly provided to increase public awareness of the S&DR legacy in this off-the-beaten-track corner of the North-East. The holy grail for the FoSDR would be for the 26 miles of former line between Witton Park and Stockton to become a World Heritage Site. To this end, the Friends have produced a series of booklets on user-friendly circular walks which draw the public's attention to surviving S&DR railway artefacts along the original route of the railway from the Durham coalfields to the Tees. The cover picture of the New Shildon specific booklet is a photograph of the Mason's Arms (now the Crossings), the building which once included an admin office and passenger waiting room for the S&DR. At the time of writing (February 2018), the pub has closed its doors and is being offered for sale. It has had a chequered history following the closure of the Wagon Works in the 1980s, which removed much of its trade. Looking at the original 'For Sale' advert for the Mason's Arms of 1835, it is apparent that many of the original features of the pub are still there today, including the extension which was once a linked granary with accommodation over the top. Recent research has identified other internal features which date from S&DR days; this despite a substantial rebuild of the building towards the end of the nineteenth century. The Mason's Arms is only one feature of Shildon's railway past that could disappear overnight unless some effort is made to preserve them. The same could be said of the former engine sheds that I had the good fortune to visit. A fate, indeed, that almost befell Hackworth's Soho Cottage and the rest of the old buildings at Locomotion.

That would be shameful. This country gave railways to the world and railways, as we know them, began in New Shildon. Locomotion attracts tens of thousands of visitors every year. In 2025, that number will increase to hundreds of thousands. Let's hope there's something left for them to see.

It is not all doom and gloom. If the G5 project may be viewed as a tribute to Shildon's railway past, then a few miles up the road is the North-East latest contribution to our national railway's future. At Newton Aycliffe, close to Heighington station, where Stephenson's *Locomotion* first raised steam, a new factory has arisen. In 2007, the government made the decision to replace the country's aging '125' train fleet and the Japanese company Hitachi, responsible for the iconic Shinkansen (Bullet Train), was given the contract. It was unclear initially where the trains would be built, or even if

The Hitachi express passenger train outside their factory at Newton Aycliffe (picture courtesy of Hitachi UK).

they would be built in the UK. Durham County Council, amongst others, set out to actively promote an area of undeveloped land east of Shildon, emphasising the area's historic links with railways. To impress a delegation of officials from Japan, who were investigating several potential sites in the UK and beyond, local developer Geoff Hunton even hired a helicopter to fly the visitors over the chosen site, now identified as in Newton Aycliffe, to provide the Japanese with a better perspective on the location, particularly its proximity to amenities including the adjacent Shildon to Darlington railway line. The fields that needed to be developed were marked out with white tape to show the location of factory buildings from the air, and hence how they would fit into the landscape. The layout and subsequent inspection by the delegation needed to be done quickly as the white tape proved irresistible to the field's ovine occupants.[79] The Hitachi team were won over and a factory costing £82 million was built, which connects to the national rail network near Heighington station. It opened its doors for business in September 2015, almost exactly 190 years after the first S&DR steam train, preceded by John Dixon, on horseback, trundled past the same site. Now fully operational, the factory employs more than

400 local people and has the capacity to build more than 35 units every month. Based on its Shinkansen forbears, the Class 800 express passenger train (IEP) has become a feature of our main lines and the factory has branched out into other novel projects including the production of commuter trains for Scotrail and intercity express trains for the Great Western Railway. The icing on the cake would be the awarding of the contract for the HS2 trains when the lines are built. What is beyond doubt is that Shildon will still be there, if needed, to meet the challenge. It is the ancestral home of the nation's railways and has nearly 200 years of local expertise to draw on. Watch this space.

The Key Players

Adamson, Daniel (1778-1832)

The landlord of the notorious Grey Horse public house in Old Shildon, a drinking venue frequented by smugglers and highwaymen in days of old. Adamson took the opportunity presented by the S&DR to operate his own horse-drawn rail passenger service between Shildon and Darlington from 1827 to 1833, after which time the S&DR took the service in-house. During the years his coach *Perseverance* worked the route, passengers bought their tickets and waited for trains in a building still standing, immediately opposite the Grey Horse. This building can therefore claim to be the world's first dedicated public railway station.

Adamson, Daniel (Jnr.) (1820-90)

The son of the above, and the thirteenth of fifteen children, suggesting his father hadn't much by way of hobbies to take up his spare time. Daniel Jnr was apprenticed to Timothy Hackworth and went on to become a draughtsman and engineer at Soho Works and eventually General Manager. After the closure of Soho Works, he set up his own business in Cheshire and achieved much success with the design of engine boilers. His company also built narrow gauge locomotives for Welsh railways, but he is perhaps best remembered for his promotion and development of the Manchester Ship Canal, of which he was eventually Company chairman.

Bouch, William (1813-76)

Bouch took over the management of the S&DR operation in conjunction with Oswald Gilkes, following the departure of Timothy Hackworth in 1840. The brother of Thomas Bouch, whose Tay Bridge notoriously collapsed in a storm killing everyone present on the train passing over it, William modernised the works at New Shildon, designing and building his own passenger and freight locomotives which, increasingly, had more in common with Robert Stephenson's engines than Hackworth's. He was instrumental in the transfer of locomotive construction to Darlington and hence the specialisation of the Shildon works towards wagon building.

He was a public benefactor to the town, overseeing for example the construction of a hospital to deal with a major smallpox outbreak in 1871. Bouch lived in Hackworth's former home, Soho Cottage, for many years after it was bought back from the Hackworth family by the S&DR. He eventually moved away to Darlington to become instrumental in establishing Darlington as the hub of the NER network in North-East England.

Dixon, John (1796-1865)

The great nephew of the surveyor Jeremiah Dixon who in 1767, accompanied by Charles Mason, carried out the first and most famous survey of the American wilderness to define the boundary between the northern and southern states, later known as the Mason-Dixon line (hence the term 'Dixieland'). A recent colleague of George Stephenson, John Dixon was a former civil clerk turned surveyor. As one of the earliest appointments of the S&DR, he assisted Stephenson in identifying the final route of the line. It was Dixon who presented Stephenson's recommendations to the proprietors of the railway. Apart from his role as surveyor to the Company he was also their financial fixer, negotiating contracts with landowners, other railways, and potential customers whilst arranging terms of employment with future employees, one of whom was Timothy Hackworth. It is reputed that it was Dixon who led the first train out of Shildon, riding on horseback and carrying a red flag. It was certainly Dixon who carried out the first survey of the land which became New Shildon.

Transferring his acquired expertise in dealing with marshland to the Liverpool and Manchester Railway (L&MR), he reunited with Stephenson to survey the swamp known as Chat Moss, that the L&MR was obliged to cross. He went on to have a distinguished career as the surveyor of choice for other new railways and, after many years away from the North-East, returned as the S&DR's Consulting Engineer in 1845, a position he retained until death.

Gilkes, Edgar (1821-94)

Born in Nailsworth, Gloucestershire, to a Quaker family, he was one of the first appointments made by his brother Oswald, after Oswald and William Bouch took over the management of the S&DR from Timothy Hackworth in 1840. Gilkes didn't stay long. After less than three years he moved to Middlesbrough to oversee the workshops which looked after the Railway's infrastructure at the Middlesbrough end of the line, including some of their rolling stock. Taking on financial partner, Isaac Wilson, he acquired workshops from the S&DR, and turned them into a specialist foundry and engineering company in Lower Commercial Street. Principally devoted to the manufacture and maintenance of steam locomotives, and now known as Gilkes, Wilson and Company, his workshops eventually built more than 350 steam locos, many of which were sold to the S&DR and the successor NER. There was to be one more unexpected and unwanted Gilkes/Bouch connection. It was Gilkes' Middlesbrough foundry which supplied the ironwork for Thomas Bouch's ill-fated Tay Bridge. The subsequent enquiry identified the substandard material used as a contributory factor in the collapse of the bridge, an accusation from which the Company never really recovered.

Gilkes, Oswald (1812-55)

Like his brother, from Gloucestershire, he was appointed by the S&DR to take over the running of the S&DR from Timothy Hackworth. Along with partner, William Bouch, he became one of the first proprietors of the Shildon Works Company. He and Bouch later acquired ownership of the operation from the S&DR, under similar terms and conditions to those of Timothy Hackworth a decade or so earlier and built several steam locomotives to Bouch's design. Although not an absolute division of their duties, it seems that Gilkes managed the finances and handled Company business on a day to day basis whilst Bouch was the forward-thinking engineer, planner and designer of rolling stock.

Glass, John (1810-84)

Born in Upleatham, Yorkshire, he was the first guard employed by the S&DR on a passenger train and one of its first employees. He started work for the Company just before the railway's opening day, at which time he was just 15 years old. It was his misfortune to be the older brother of the first person recorded as killed on a public railway; this taking place at Witton Park Colliery. Along with Timothy Hackworth and Thomas MacNay, Glass was fundamental in the creation of the local Railway Institute to the great benefit of the local community. In his address to the Institute on the first anniversary of its creation he declared:

> 'I was present when the first rail was laid in this town. I saw the construction, the opening day, the first locomotive, the horse coaches and many other things connected with our early history.'

Self-taught, by 1871 he was the accountant for the NER's works at New Shildon.

Graham, John (1799-1864)

The appointment of John Graham to the role of Traffic Manager in 1831 was a major step forward for the young S&DR. In the first place it took much weight off Timothy Hackworth, allowing him to concentrate on improving the design and construction of the engines under his control. More importantly, Graham was encouraged to keep comprehensive details of daily events on the railway, thereby identifying important improvements and correcting potential problems before they were beyond rectification, particularly those pertaining to safe working practice. Graham had started his working life down the pit at the age of 10, like George Stephenson operating trapdoors which controlled airflow. He was based at Hetton Colliery when he applied for work at the S&DR and may therefore have been recommended to Edward Pease by Stephenson who had designed the colliery railway and supplied their steam locomotives. Whilst employed by the S&DR he also acted as Mining Engineer for Pease and Partners, another company owned by the Pease family. He is buried in St. John's churchyard, Shildon, next to the man whose career he did so much to define, Timothy Hackworth.

Greener, Thomas (1786-1853)

Thomas saw the first rails of the S&DR laid at Stockton. He got the contract to build the cuttings and embankments of Etherley Incline and became the first engineman on the Etherley stationary engine. His biographer, John Glass, reported in respect of the upkeep of the Etherley engine:

> 'He (*Greener*) was also very particular in having the polished work kept shining bright, and the flooring kept very clean. This beautiful engine was often visited by ladies and gentlemen in the neighbourhood who mostly expressed their great satisfaction at this masterpiece of human skill, and the interesting conversation of the engineer.'

Thomas is said to have controversially decorated his Etherley Engine House with hand painted caricatures of local people. He left the S&DR c.1827 and was succeeded by his brother John, who was later sadly killed under the beam of the engine in 1843. Thomas, along with Timothy Hackworth and Robert Young of Brusselton, was responsible for the construction of the Methodist chapels in the Shildon area. During the construction of the Liverpool & Manchester Railway(L&MR) he worked for his former Killingworth colleague, George Stephenson, on the difficult construction of the railway over Chat Moss. He came back to work on the S&DR and helped to build the staithes at Middlesbrough (designed by Hackworth), and later worked on the construction of the London & Croydon, Whitby & Pickering and London and Blackwall Railways. He died in London on 11 January 1852.

Hackworth, Timothy (1786-1850)

Like George Stephenson, a son of Wylam, he started work as assistant to his father, who was senior blacksmith at Wylam Colliery until his death in 1804. Timothy completed his apprenticeship there and in 1810, like his father, was appointed Senior Blacksmith. His employer, the colliery owner Christopher Blackett, had earlier (1805) authorised the construction of a Trevithick designed steam locomotive but rejected it because he thought it too heavy for his flimsy colliery rails. On appointing a new Viewer (for Viewer read Pit Manager), William Hedley, Blackett committed to steam technology, authorising experiments in steam locomotion, beginning with rail/ wheel adhesion trials in 1811. Blackett's idea was to replace the horses currently used for shifting coal from his colliery to the nearest navigable part of the River Tyne at Lemington, since horses in war time were expensive to obtain and maintain. Hackworth took an active part in the locomotive experiments and had direct involvement in the construction of at least three of the revolutionary steam locomotives built there, including the world-famous *Puffing Billy*. Whilst working on sister engine *Wylam Dilly*, Hackworth fell out with Hedley over his being expected to work on the engines on the sabbath, which conflicted with Hackworth's strict Methodist principles. He therefore left Blackett's employ and was later appointed foreman smith at Walbottle Colliery. It was while he was there he went as a borrowed man to assist George Stephenson at his engineering works in Forth Street, Newcastle. During his brief period at Forth Street, Hackworth almost certainly contributed to the building of *Locomotion No. 1* (then called *Active*) and was Stephenson's man on the ground during the building of the stationary engines at Brusselton and Etherley. In 1825 he was appointed Railway Superintendent of the S&DR and used the engineering skills acquired at Wylam to produce the first reliable locomotive for his new employer, *Royal George*. Drawing upon the favourable atmosphere generated by the performance of *Royal George*, Hackworth went on to build many more engines both for the S&DR and other railway companies, particularly after he had established his own factory at Shildon, later known as Soho Works. He was a formidable engineer, his technical innovations including, but not limited to, a refined form of blast pipe, whose draught inducing principle he was the first to quantify. He also invented the cast iron 'plug' wheels, with wrought iron tyres, which proved so much more robust than the spoked wheels used on Stephenson's engines. He never received in his lifetime the claim or adulation his engineering prowess deserved. His 0-4-0 engine *Sanspareil*, built in his spare time and on a shoestring, was the only engine to give Stephenson's *Rocket* a run for its money at the Rainhill Trials and he and his brother Thomas constructed the first locomotive to operate on a conventional railway in Russia. He parted company with the S&DR in 1840 ostensibly to revive the fortunes of his own Soho Works, but that Company never generated much in the way of profits in the ten years he had overall control. He died from typhus in 1850.

Hackworth, Thomas (1797-1877)

The younger brother of Timothy by eleven years, he had almost the same engineering grounding as his elder sibling, being similarly apprenticed at Wylam Colliery during the period the steam locomotives were being built. It was his later claim that he made parts for all those engines in the blacksmith shop and assisted in their assembly. It was also Thomas who replaced his brother as foreman smith at Walbottle Colliery after Timothy's secondment to Forth Street. When his brother established his own engineering works at Shildon, Thomas was therefore the logical choice to run the Company on Timothy's behalf. He successfully managed Soho Works and the associated manufactory Hackworth and Downing for five years, but left, seemingly under a cloud, at the end of 1839 to set up business in Stockton with a new partner, George Fossick. Fossick and Hackworth duly flourished, producing as many as 100 new locomotives for railway companies and collieries across the British Isles, including Ireland. Whilst at Stockton he began the Company's transition to steamship engine manufacture which would supersede any railway related industry. The firm of Fossick and Hackworth made the ships' engines used on a number of confederate warships during the American Civil war. He retired in 1865, by which time the Company had established an international reputation as the producer of sturdy and reliable ship's engines. Renamed Blair and Co, after the talented Scottish engineer Thomas had appointed manager, it went on to become the biggest employer in Stockton until its closure nearly a century later. Thomas left the North-East and moved to Newton Abbott, in Devon, perhaps with half an eye on resurrecting his railway career with the Great Western Railway which had also recently set up home in that town. Alas it was not to be.

Hackworth-Young, Jane (b. 1948) (born Jane Ann Young)

Daughter of Reginald Hackworth Young and hence great-great-grand daughter of Timothy Hackworth, no-one has done more to save and promote the railway heritage of Shildon. Jane was formerly Secretary/PA to Donald Albery of The Wyndham Theatres Ltd, London, eventually joining the British Theatre Association to become its Director. In 1992 she spent two terms as a Labour Councillor for the Borough of Hammersmith & Fulham and worked as Administrator for the Russian European Trust before settling in Teesdale in 2002, just 20 miles from her forebear's home in Shildon. She became involved in the campaign to save Shildon's railway heritage and still remains the town's most vociferous advocate in that context. This led to 45 years of research on the Stockton & Darlington Railway and her own Hackworth/ Young family. Jane catalogued the surviving Hackworth family documents, which provide unique first-hand accounts of the trials and tribulations of the S&DR's early years. These are now at the Search Engine at the NRM at York. Jane is a popular figure at Locomotion, giving regular talks to schoolchildren and fronting local events, particularly those related to the first years of the S&DR. Latterly she has also become an active Trustee of the Friends of the Stockton and Darlington Railway, whose aim is to ensure the survival of what remains of the S&DR, particularly along the course of the first 26 miles from Witton Park over the inclines to Shildon and then on to Stockton, with the ultimate outcome being that the original line is given World Heritage status. One element of S&DR history close to her heart was the Company's use of numbered plaques to identify domestic housing within their ownership. Jane has spent years identifying which of these properties have survived, whether the S&DR house plaques still exist, and where they are located.

MacNay (also spelt McNay and occasionally Mac Nay), Thomas (1810-69)

Born in Wallsend, he was apprenticed at Hawthorn's engineering works at Newcastle and joined Timothy Hackworth at Shildon in October 1832, as the storeman. He later became the Company's clerk/ draughtsman. He was appointed Secretary of the S&DR in 1849. Self-educated, he was one of the leading lights in the establishment of the Shildon Railway Institute, and the most vocal proponent of Shildon's first library. In endeavouring to sell the library idea to the S&DR, who he had hoped would finance the enterprise, he wrote:

> 'The Shildon Library is intended for the promotion of useful knowledge and the promoters of this Institute, being deeply impressed with the numerous advantages derivable from learning, have been induced to establish a library for the benefit of the inhabitants of Shildon and its vicinity; hoping that through the books connected therewith and the lectures delivered thereat, practical knowledge may be extensively disseminated and perpetuated to generations yet unborn.'

After spells as the Secretary of the Auckland and Weardale, Wear Valley and Middlesbrough branches of the NER, he ended his days as Secretary of the Railway's Darlington branch. One of his most significant contributions to rail safety was to introduce the block signalling system across the network, which prevented two trains entering the same section of line at any one time.

Nunn, Walter (1920-2007)

Educated at Bishop Auckland Grammar School, Walter started his working life as a welder at Shildon Wagon Works and became Senior Welding Instructor at the Technical College. He was a Labour Party Member for 70 years, Shildon Branch Secretary for 54, Councillor for 47 and an honorary alderman. In 2007, at a dinner in his honour, speaker after speaker praised his honesty. Walter and his wife, Kathy (the sister of the famous local radical writer, Sid Chaplin), opened their door to everyone 24 hours a day. Walter's desire to bring the names of Shildon and Timothy Hackworth to the public was unfailing. When it appeared that the Hackworth family home,

Soho House, at Shildon, and the remaining adjacent buildings were going to be demolished to make way for a new road, he was the key local representative to support the campaign to save them. As Chair of Shildon Council he was one of the first supporters of the concept of a railway heritage town with Soho Cottage as its centre and when Sedgefield District Council was formed he lobbied the Council to put Shildon 'on the map'. He lived to see the railway buildings incorporated in 2004 into Locomotion at Shildon.

Pease, Edward (1767-1857)

Recently retired from his own business as a Darlington wool merchant, in 1818 he attempted to revive interest in a scheme proposed five years earlier to build a canal from the South Durham coalfield to the River Tees at Stockton. Along with other potential investors he commissioned a survey of the best possible routes for either a canal or some sort of horse-powered tramroad of the type already part of the north-east landscape. The economics of the tramroad, after being elevated to full railway status, won out. Further surveys were commissioned, this time specifically for a railway from the collieries near Witton Park to the nearest port on the Tees at Stockton, albeit routed through his home town of Darlington. Not long after the Company's railway proposal of 1821 was approved by parliament, Pease met George Stephenson, the country's leading advocate for steam railways, and was invited to observe Stephenson's engines at work at Killingworth. On the strength of this visit, he resubmitted an amended railway proposal to parliament, this time specifically allowing for the use of steam locos. Stephenson was invited to resurvey the route of the line, previously surveyed by George Overton, and the rest is history. Unfortunately, Pease was absent on what should have been his greatest day, the day *Locomotion No.1* made the first journey from New Shildon to Stockton, as his youngest son Isaac had sadly died the same morning. With no template to work from Pease had created the world's first locomotive operated public railway and put his home town of Darlington on the world map. It was Edward Pease who provided much of the funding for the construction of Stephenson's locomotive works at Forth Street, Newcastle, and Pease remained Stephenson's loyal friend for the rest of his long life.

Pease, Joseph (1799-1872)

Son of Edward Pease, he was the most active Pease family participant in the development of the S&DR. Once the railway was up and running it was Joseph who represented the proprietors at Committee meetings and authorised major appointments and expenditure. A frequent visitor to Shildon, he was one of the party of dignitaries aboard a coach in the process of being hauled up Brusselton incline when the rope broke and in the end he was lucky to escape with his life. He was also in the first party of officials to travel through the Shildon tunnel before its official opening in 1842. He became joint owner of many collieries who were customers of the S&DR. The town of Middlesbrough owes Joseph a special debt of gratitude because he was fundamental in its creation, arranging the purchase of the unpromising marshland beside the Tees which became the town. Once the port of Middlesbrough had been established he oversaw the move to Middlesbrough from Stockton as the favoured freight terminal for his railway. In later years he became an MP. It is a measure of his national status that he was able to take his place at Westminster without providing the normal statutory oaths of allegiance to the Crown, which conflicted with his Quaker beliefs, something previously unheard of.

Stephenson, George (1781-1848)

What more is there to say about George Stephenson? Often acknowledged as the greatest railwayman of them all, Stephenson's is certainly the greatest and the most moving rags-to-riches story. Born to a Wylam family who occupied just one room in a tied colliery cottage, he ended his days in his own stately home in Chesterfield. George's father was a fireman (the person responsible for tending the fires in the boilers) at Wylam Colliery and George himself spent time underground, as a child, working the shutters that controlled the movement of fresh air through the pit. From an early age he was interested in all things mechanical and taught himself the rudiments of engineering. Always a tinkerer, he took machines apart to see how they worked and thereby determined how they might be improved. Railways were part of his life from the beginning. The privately owned Wylam Colliery railway ran past his one-roomed home and, although he had moved away by the time the Wylam experiments in steam were taking place, he nevertheless made a nuisance of himself, returning frequently to witness the breakthroughs being made, to the point he was eventually barred from the colliery before he got chance to see the breakthrough in the locomotive experiments, *Puffing Billy*. It was fortunate that his interest and enthusiasm for steam engines was shared by his new employer at Killingworth Colliery, where he used the knowledge acquired to build a succession of experimental locomotives, each one an improvement on its predecessor. He gained a reputation for engineering skill and was invited to design and build engines for Hetton Colliery, along with the construction of the Company's private railway from the colliery to the dockside on the River Wear. When he heard that the S&DR had been given parliamentary approval he arranged to visit the proprietor, Edward Pease, walking the length of the proposed route on the day of the meeting to determine how much work was likely to be involved. Impressed by both Stephenson's enthusiasm and, after a visit to Killingworth, his engines, he was appointed principal engineer for the new railway, with resurveying the route of the line his first task. With interest in steam locomotion dwindling nationally, Stephenson managed to convince Edward Pease that horses represented the past and steam the future. Provided with finance from his new employer he built his own loco factory at Newcastle, where *Locomotion No. 1* was built. Many of the engines used by the S&DR were subsequently built there. He was a great innovator and experimenter, fiddling with designs until he got them right. Whilst working at Killingworth Colliery, for example, he invented a miner's safety lamp which became standard in north-east England. It is said that the term 'Geordie', meaning north-east people, has its origins in the 'Geordie lamp' carried by miners. One of Stephenson's notable contributions to the S&DR was his promotion of the 'dandy cart' which gave a new lease of life to horse-drawn trains. The S&DR, for Stephenson however, was merely a stepping stone to greater things, most notably the Liverpool and Manchester Railway, which Stephenson engineered. He worked on many more railway projects throughout the country and his enthusiasm for steam never wavered. He wasn't perfect. Despite a natural talent for understanding machines he was not a great theoretical engineer, often being held back by a lack of education, oratory and literacy skills. He worked by trial and error and it often took others with more formal education, particularly his son Robert, to identify and correct the problems that often haunted his engines. Nevertheless, his contribution to the story of railways cannot be overestimated. He was the principal advocate for steam when the rest of the world was largely turning its back. Without George the development of railways would, at best, have stagnated for decades and, at worst, remained the niche curiosity it was before his intervention.

Stephenson, Robert (1803-59)

Born at Willington Quay near Newcastle, after the death of his mother and baby sister, he lived with an aunt in Scotland before joining his father who had moved to Killingworth, where George was colliery engineer. Unlike his dad, Robert had been provided with a formal education, specialising in engineering, the cost of which his father underwrote. When the S&DR made the decision to use steam locomotives on its railway, the Company bankrolled George Stephenson's new engine works at Newcastle, and the management was handed to Robert, who was only 22 at the time. Just after work began on the construction of *Locomotion*, however, Robert took off on a sabbatical to Colombia to engineer the first major railway project in that country. It didn't work out and after three years he returned to the UK, but not before he had met and repatriated Richard Trevithick whose similar overseas adventure had come to nothing and was destitute. Robert arrived home just after his father was appointed engineer of the Liverpool and Manchester Railway and resumed control of Forth Street, building engines to his own and Hackworth's design for the S&DR. For the Rainhill Trials, Robert designed the revolutionary *Rocket*, the engine that eventually triumphed. Robert could point to many other major achievements in his lifetime: for example, he engineered the London and Birmingham Railway: the Britannia Bridge over the Menai Straits to Anglesey and the High Level Bridge over the Tyne in his native Newcastle. It wasn't all plain sailing. A few months after his wife died his new house burnt down and he lost his most precious possessions, including all the mementoes of their marriage. He also, through no fault of his own, became embroiled in a bankruptcy scandal involving a railway he once helped to engineer, the Stanhope and Tyne. Better spoken and better educated than his father, he was well thought of in the corridors of power and amongst his peers. He was offered and declined a knighthood, but nevertheless received many honours right across Europe and fully deserves his reputation as one of this country's greatest Victorian engineers.

Storey, Thomas (1789-1859)

Storey's involvement with the S&DR followed a similar pattern to John Dixon's. Related by marriage to George Stephenson he took part in the initial survey, working alongside both Dixon and Stephenson. Like Dixon he became the railway's surveyor, with his name prominent on the bottom of many of the contracts signed by the Company during its first years of operation. It was Storey who organised the sale of the Mason's Arms in 1835, the only indication we have that that famous pub, once the admin office for the S&DR, may originally have been in the ownership of the railway company. A company of Storey's also supplied the first chaldron wagons used on the S&DR. He was a more than competent architect. Storey designed one of the world's first skew arch bridges for the Company's Hagger Leases branch line and he was the engineer responsible for the design and construction of the Shildon tunnel. In 1836 he left the S&DR to join the Great North of England Railway, surveying the route that would become today's main line between York and Darlington. His career nosedived after some of the bridges he had designed on the main line collapsed and he ended his life as the owner of a small foundry in St. Helens, Auckland.

Young, Reginald Hackworth (1905-77)

Great grandson of Timothy Hackworth and a distinguished engineer, being a Bachelor of Science in Engineering, a Member of The Institute of Electrical Engineers, The Institute of Mechanical Engineers and The Institute of Heating & Ventilating Engineers. He designed the first cooker with electric oven and gas hobs for English Electric. He became Superintendent Mechanical and Electrical Engineer of the Ministry of Public Buildings and Works (later the DOE), and was sufficiently familiar with the trappings of government, both national and local, to know the right levers to pull to get things done when it came to a campaign to save Shildon's railway heritage. In 1972, Rex as he was normally known, accompanied by daughter Jane, visited Shildon ostensibly to try and achieve recognition for his great grandfather. It was a timely moment as much, if not all, of Shildon's railway heritage was on the brink of being lost due to an ill considered new road proposal. However, through his tireless campaigning the surviving early railway buildings, including Soho Cottage, were saved for the nation along with a formal acknowledgement of Timothy's legacy to the town. The opening of the Hackworth Museum and the eventual donation of the family's papers to the National Railway Museum made a significant contribution to the creation of Locomotion at Shildon, although Rex would not live to see it. He was tragically killed in a car accident in 1977.

Locomotives built at New Shildon

Locomotive	Date built	Designer	Customer	Type	Origin
Royal George (rebuild)	1827	Timothy Hackworth	S&DR	0-6-0	Shildon Works
Victory	1829	Timothy Hackworth	S&DR	0-6-0	Shildon Works
Sanspareil	1829	Timothy Hackworth	L&MR	0-4-0	Shildon Works
Majestic	1831	Timothy Hackworth	S&DR	0-6-0	Shildon Works
Coronation	1831	Timothy Hackworth	S&DR	0-6-0	Shildon Works
William the Fourth	1831	Timothy Hackworth	S&DR	0-6-0	Shildon Works
Northumbrian	1831	Timothy Hackworth	S&DR	0-6-0	Shildon Works
Lord Brougham	1832	Timothy Hackworth	S&DR	0-6-0	Shildon Works
Shildon	1832	Timothy Hackworth	S&DR	0-6-0	Shildon Works
Magnet	1835	Timothy Hackworth	S&DR	0-6-0	Soho Works
(Unidentified)	1836	Timothy Hackworth	Deanery Colliery	0-6-0	Soho Works
(Unnamed Russian engine)	1836	Robert Stephenson	Russian Government	2-2-2	Soho Works
Arrow	1837	(Stephenson?)	S&DR	2-2-2	Soho Works
Beehive	1837	Timothy Hackworth	S&DR	0-6-0	Soho Works
Samson	1838	Timothy Hackworth	Stellarton Rlwy, Canada	0-6-0	Soho Works
Hercules	1838	Timothy Hackworth	Stellarton Rlwy, Canada	0-6-0	Soho Works
John Buddle	1838	Timothy Hackworth	Stellarton Rlwy, Canada	0-6-0	Soho Works
Tory	1838	Timothy Hackworth	S&DR	0-6-0	Soho Works
Whig	1838	Timothy Hackworth	S&DR	0-6-0	Soho Works
Victoria	1839	Timothy Hackworth	Llanelly Rlwy & Dock Co.	0-6-0	Soho Works
Albert	1839	Timothy Hackworth	Llanelly Rlwy & Dock Co.	0-6-0	Soho Works

Locomotive	Date built	Designer	Customer	Type	Origin
Despatch	1839	Timothy Hackworth	S&DR	0-6-0	Soho Works
Auckland	1839	Timothy Hackworth	S&DR	0-6-0	Soho Works
Coxhoe	1840	Timothy Hackworth	Clarence Railway	0-6-0	Soho Works
Evenwood	1840	Timothy Hackworth	Clarence Railway	0-6-0	Soho Works
Buddle	1840	Timothy Hackworth	S.Hetton Coal Co.	0-6-0	Soho Works
Kellor	1840	Timothy Hackworth	S.Hetton Coal Co.	0-6-0	Soho Works
Washington	1840	Timothy Hackworth	S.Hetton Coal Co.	0-6-0	Soho Works
Prince Albert	1840	Timothy Hackworth	S.Hetton Coal Co.	0-6-0	Soho Works
unidentified	1840	Timothy Hackworth			Soho Works
Dart	1840	Timothy Hackworth	S&DR	0-4-0	Soho Works
Prince	1842	W.Bouch	S&DR	0-6-0	Shildon Works Co.
Leader	1842	Timothy Hackworth	S&DR	0-6-0	Soho Works
Briton	1842	Timothy Hackworth	S&DR	0-6-0	Soho Works
John	1842	Timothy Hackworth	Seghill Colliery	0-6-0	Soho Works
Meteor	1843	W.Bouch	S&DR	2-2-2	Shildon Works Co.
Miner	1845	W.Bouch	S&DR	0-6-0	Shildon Works Co.
Wear	1845	W.Bouch	S&DR	0-6-0	Shildon Works Co.
Redcar	1845	W.Bouch	S&DR	0-6-0	Shildon Works Co.
Samson	1845	Timothy Hackworth	Seghill Colliery	0-6-0	Soho Works
no.52	1845	John Gray	L.B.& S.C.R	2-2-2	Soho Works
no.53	1846	John Gray	L.B.& S.C.R	2-2-2	Soho Works
no.54	1846	John Gray	L.B.& S.C.R	2-2-2	Soho Works
Eldon	1846	W.Bouch	S&DR	0-6-0	Shildon Works Co.
Shildon	1846	W.Bouch	S&DR	0-6-0	Shildon Works Co.
Driver	1846	W.Bouch	S&DR	0-6-0	Shildon Works Co.
Commerce	1847	W.Bouch	S&DR	0-6-0	Shildon Works Co.
Guisboro	1847	W.Bouch	S&DR	0-6-0	Shildon Works Co.
Walsingham (rebuild)	1847	W.Bouch	S&DR	0-6-0	Shildon Works Co.
Gem	1847	W.Bouch	S&DR	0-6-0	Shildon Works Co.

Locomotive	Date built	Designer	Customer	Type	Origin
Rokeby	1847	W.Bouch	S&DR	0-6-0	Shildon Works Co.
Ruby	1847	W.Bouch	S&DR	0-6-0	Shildon Works Co.
no.55	1847	John Gray	L.B.& S.C.R	2-2-2	Soho Works
no.56	1847	John Gray	L.B.& S.C.R	2-2-2	Soho Works
no.57	1847	John Gray	L.B.& S.C.R	2-2-2	Soho Works
no.58	1847	John Gray	L.B.& S.C.R	2-2-2	Soho Works
no.59	1847	John Gray	L.B.& S.C.R	2-2-2	Soho Works
no.60	1847	John Gray	L.B.& S.C.R	2-2-2	Soho Works
no.50	1848	John Gray	L.B.& S.C.R	2-2-2	Soho Works
no.51	1848	John Gray	L.B.& S.C.R	2-2-2	Soho Works
no.49	1848	John Gray	L.B.& S.C.R	2-2-2	Soho Works
no.52	1848	John Gray	L.B.& S.C.R	2-2-2	Soho Works
no.55	1848	John Gray	L.B.& S.C.R	2-2-2	Soho Works
Sanspareil No.2	1848	Timothy Hackworth	show engine	2-2-2	Soho Works
Birkbeck	1849	W.Bouch	S&DR	0-6-0	Shildon Works Co.
Larchfield	1849	W.Bouch	S&DR	0-6-0	Shildon Works Co.
no.1	1849	Timothy Hackworth	Clarence Railway	0-6-0	Soho Works
no.2	1849/1850	Timothy Hackworth	Clarence Railway	0-4-0	Soho Works
no.3	1849/1850	Timothy Hackworth	Clarence Railway	0-4-0	Soho Works
no.4	1849/1850	Timothy Hackworth	Clarence Railway	0-6-0	Soho Works
no.7	1849/1850	Timothy Hackworth	Clarence Railway	0-6-0	Soho Works
Seymour	1849/1850	Timothy Hackworth	Clarence Railway	0-6-0	Soho Works
Pilot	1849/1850	Timothy Hackworth	Clarence Railway	0-6-0	Soho Works
no.13	1849/1850	Timothy Hackworth	Clarence Railway	0-6-0	Soho Works
Duke	1854	Bouch/Gilkes	S&DR	0-6-0	Shildon Works Co.
Ayton	1855	Bouch/Gilkes	S&DR	2-4-0	Shildon Works Co.
Stobart	1855	Bouch/Gilkes	S&DR	0-6-0	Shildon Works Co.
Eden	1855	Bouch/Gilkes	S&DR	0-6-0	Shildon Works Co.

Locomotive	Date built	Designer	Customer	Type	Origin
Gladstone	1863	W.Bouch	NER	0-6-0	Shildon Works Co.
Barrow	1863	W.Bouch	NER	0-6-0	Shildon Works Co.
London	1864	W.Bouch	NER	0-6-0	Shildon Works Co.
Contractor	1864	W.Bouch	NER	0-6-0	Shildon Works Co.
John Dixon	1864	W.Bouch	NER	0-6-0	Shildon Works Co.
no.2 (later NER 1002)	1865	W.Bouch	NER	0-6-0	Shildon Works Co.
no.3 (later NER 1003)	1865	W.Bouch	NER	0-6-0	Shildon Works Co.
Spring	1865	W.Bouch	NER	0-6-0	Shildon Works Co.
Summer	1865	W.Bouch	NER	0-6-0	Shildon Works Co.
no.56 (later NER 1056)	1866	W.Bouch	NER	0-6-0	Shildon Works Co.
no.57 (later NER 1057)	1866	W.Bouch	NER	0-6-0	Shildon Works Co.
Winter	1866	W.Bouch	NER	0-6-0	Shildon Works Co.
Alice	1866	W.Bouch	NER	0-6-0	Shildon Works Co.
Helena	1866	W.Bouch	NER	0-6-0	Shildon Works Co.
Ireland	1867	W.Bouch	NER	0-6-0	Shildon Works Co.
England	1867	W.Bouch	NER	0-6-0	Shildon Works Co.

In addition, four new engines are known to have been authorised in 1870 for construction at Shildon, but they do not appear in official listings and are therefore difficult to separate from other NER engines built at the same time at Darlington. (There were at least a dozen 0-6-0s built for the NER in that year whose place of manufacturer is not identified in the *British Railway Catalogue 1825-1923*.)

Bibliography

AHRONS E.L. *The British Steam Locomotive* (The Locomotive Publishing Company Ltd.:1927)

APPLEBY K.C. *Shildon-Newport in Retrospect* (RCTS:1990)

BAXTER B. *British Locomotive Catalogue 1825 -1923 Vol.5A* (Moorland Publishing Company:1986)

CORKIN R. *Shildon -Cradle of the Railways* (Frank Graham:1977)

EMETT C. *The Stockton and Darlington Railway 175 Years* (Sutton Publishing:2000)

GRAHAM G. *Notes of Incidents Connected with the Stockton and Darlington Rlwy* (National Archive ref. RAIL 667/427)

GRIFFITHS R. and SMITH P. *The Directory of British Engine Sheds: 2* (Oxford Publishing Co:2000)

HEWISON C.H. *Locomotive Boiler Explosions* (David and Charles:1983)

HOLMES P.J. *Stockton and Darlington Railway 1825 – 1975* (First Avenue Publishing Company: undated)

HOOLE K. *North Eastern Locomotive Sheds* (David and Charles:1972)

HOOLE K. *Stockton and Darlington Railway – Anniversary Celebrations of the World's First Steam-worked Public Railway* (Dalesman Books:1974)

JEANS J.S. *History of the Stockton and Darlington Railway* (Originally published Longman, Green and Co:1875, this source the 3rd Edition (Scolar Press Ltd.:1974)

LAWSON F. *Shildon.* Series of seven books (self-published:2001)

LOWE J.W. *British Steam Locomotive Builders* (Goose and Son:1975)

MCCORMICK B. *The Peases and the S&DR Railway* (Bermac Publications:2008)

OEYNHAUSEN C.Von and DECHEN H.Von *Railways in England 1826 and 1827* (The Newcomen Society:1971)

REVERERS *Three Steam to Shildon* (6b6 Photographic:1976)

SKEAT W.O. *George Stephenson – The Engineer and His Letters* (The Institute of Mechanical Engineers:1973)

SLACK G. *The First Five Miles* (Addo Printing Ltd.:2015)

SLACK G. *Shildon – the World's First Railway Town – The Early Years*(GSL Publishing:2017)

SPEDDING R. *Shildon Works – a working man's life* (Durham CC:1988)

TOMLINSON W.W. *Tomlinson's North Eastern Railway* 3rd Edition (David and Charles:1987)

Yeadons Register of LNER locomotives Vol. 38 (Challenger and Book Law Publications:2005)

YOUNG R. *Timothy Hackworth and the Locomotive* 3rd reprint (The Hackworth Society:2000)

It would also be unfair to exclude the Ian Allan 'abc' series of listed 'British Locomotives', the recent informative series of S&DR related walks leaflets published by the 'Friends of the Stockton and Darlington Railway' and historical papers on Shildon and the S&DR produced by Andy Guy and Dieter Hopkin for the Early Railways conferences.

Other relevant documents
1) Hopkin D. 'Timothy Hackworth and the Soho Works 1830 – 1850'
2) Walker Thomas M. 'Thomas Greener and a Model Steam Engine'.

Acknowledgements
1) The National Archive at Kew
2) Jane Hackworth-Young for permission to use certain illustrations and for much relevant background detail.

Notes

1. S&DR sub-committee report 1 July 1825
2. *Northern Echo* 31 May 1881
3. Hackworth archive 'Hack 1-1-24'
4. Works subcommittee report dated 8 July 1836
5. Source - Ancestry UK
6. S&DR 'caution' notice to enginemen dated 7 November 1831.
7. Hewison, *Locomotive Boiler Explosions* p.102
8. S&DR works subcommittee report 1 July 1825
9. *The Directory of British Engine Sheds* (North Midlands, Northern England and Scotland) p.317
10. See RAIL 667/129 Shildon Works Report 8 May 1840.
11. See p.79 of Ken Hoole's book *North Eastern Locomotive Sheds*
12. *Timothy Hackworth and the Locomotive* p.156
13. Holmes P.J. *Stockton and Darlington Railway 1825 – 1975* p.20
14. Works committee report 27 September 1833
15. S&DR order (signatory Richard Otley) titled 'Cautions to Enginemen, wagon and coach drivers, etc' dated 7 November 1831.
16. Hopkins D. *Timothy Hackworth and the Soho Works 1830 – 1850*
17. Source – 1977 letter from Arthur Stabler whose grandfather worked at Soho Works as a blacksmith.
18. Works committee report 27 September 1839.
19. Works Committee minutes 25 October 1839.
20. *British Locomotive Catalogue*, Volume 5A pages 74 to 77
21. Shildon Works Company minutes 9 October 1843.
22. Works Committee minutes 4 July 1845
23. Works Committee minutes 2 January 1846
24. 1933 Shildon Railway Institute Centenary booklet: p.11
25. Shildon Works Committee report 10 February 1841
26. Shildon Works Committee minutes 14 July 1841
27. Shildon Works Committee minutes 19 June 1846
28. *Northern Echo* 10 January 2007.
29. Shildon Works Committee minutes 2 October 1846
30. Shildon Works Committee reports 21 January 1846
31. *British Locomotive Catalogue* Vol 5A p.78

32. *Northern Echo* 19 November 1897
33. *Durham County Advertiser* 25 February 1835.
34. Lawson F. *Shildon and District – a Miscellany* p.270
35. *Middlesbrough Daily Gazette* 26 December 1884
36. Hardie C. 'FoSDR Shildon circular walk leaflet (3)' (2017)
37. Hackworth family Archive - Hack 1-1-34
38. Hackworth Archive 'Hack 1-1-41'
39. *Durham Chronicle* 10 February 1854.
40. Shildon Works report 11 October 1840.
41. Shildon Works Company minutes 6 June 1845
42. Source - The Shildon Railway Institute centennial report of 1933
43. Tomlinson's *North Eastern Railway* p.609 onwards.
44. From Charles Dickens *Dombey and Son* published 1848
45. Allen C.J. *The North Eastern Railway* p.146
46. Annual 'Reports of Sub Inspectors of Railways on Accidents' (North Eastern Railway)
47. Minutes of 'Congres International des Chemins de Fer - Troisieme Session - 1889'.
48. Richard Pickering's wagon department report for Shildon 11 August 1853
49. *Northern Echo* 8 November 1875. The distinction between wagons and trucks isn't clear.
50. Lawson – *Shildon and District, a Miscellany Part 1* p.8
51. Spedding R, *Shildon Wagon Works – A working man's life* (Durham CC:1988)
52. Lawson – *Shildon 1935 – 1975* p.3
53. Lawson – *Shildon 1935 -1975* p.79
54. Spedding R – *Shildon Wagon Works – A working man's life* pages 10-13
55. Lawson: *Shildon 1939-1975.*
56. RAIL 667/33
57. *Northern Echo* 8 February 1881
58. Lawson F. *Shildon 1800 -1914* pages 20/21
59. National Archive RAIL 667/146
60. Amalgamated Society of Railway Servants
61. Staley's story is drawn from an article by Christine Jemmeson in the February 2018 edition of *The Journal of the North Eastern Railway Association*
62. Corkin R. *Shildon Cradle of the Railways* p. 10
63. Corkin R. *Shildon Cradle of the Railways* p.11

64. Various sources including, surprisingly, the *Belfast Newsletter* of 22 August 1911

65. *Hartlepool Northern Daily Mail* 23 August 1911.

66. *Yorkshire Evening Post* 30 September 1919: *Dundee Courier* 4 May 1926

67. *Yorkshire Post and Leeds Intelligencer* 11 August 1930, *Leeds Mercury* 25 June 1932.

68. Lawson F. *Shildon 1935 – 1975* 'War and Economic Change' p.72

69. Appleby K.C. *Shildon-Newport in retrospect* p.74

70. *Hartlepool Northern Daily Mail*, 4 November 1919.

71. Hoole K. *Stockton and Darlington Railway* p.44.

72. *Belfast Newsletter* 6 May 1929

73. *Aberdeen Press and Journal* 2 July 1925

74. Source of engines and order in parade, *Steam to Shildon* (6b6 Photographic:1976)

75. *Daily Express* 1 September 1975.

76. *Leeds Mercury* 21 December 1923

77. Lawson: *Shildon 1939 -1975*

78. e.g. Mountford C. *The Private Railways of County Durham* p.311

79. *Northern Echo* 21 May 2014

Index